The Darkside Dichotomy

The Darkside Dichotomy: Unleashing Your True Power Through Pain

All Rights Reserved

COPYRIGHT © 2019 Aaron Nash

This book may not be reproduced, transmitted, or stored in whole or in part by any means, including graphic, electronic, or mechanical without the express written consent of the publisher except in the case of brief questions embodied in critical articles and reviews.

ISBN: 9781086774269

Cover design by Sooraj Mathew

Edited by Hilary Jastram

iii BOOKMARK

Dedication

This book is dedicated to the people in our lives who contributed to our negative emotions.

This book is dedicated to the financier who backed out on me the week before closing on my business. Without you, I would not have learned courage, resilience and resourcefulness.

This book is dedicated to my father, who left my mother and his two sons with nothing. It taught me to grow up expecting nothing from anyone; it taught me the traits I want to make sure my kids see in me; it taught me that giving up affects others far more than the person who gives up.

This book is dedicated to all those who doubted me, the ones who told me I was running away to Florida, the ones who told me I needed a back-up plan, the ones who rolled their eyes when I told them what I was going to become, the ones who tried to hold me back with hate, and a scarcity, and small-town mindset.

This book is dedicated to all the "investment" owners in fitness, without you, I never would've had the drive, desire, and passion to change an industry that fails its clients more than it helps them succeed. Without you, I wouldn't have been able to succeed so rapidly due to your lack of work ethic, passion for the industry, and culture created for your teams.

This book is dedicated to all the people who root for you until you pass them and then look at you like you're the asshole for never settling and accepting a life just below theirs.

This book is dedicated to anyone who looks at someone successful with disdain instead of respect and a willingness to learn.

This book is dedicated to the addictions I allowed to control me and use to get pity from others who never pushed me. Without you, I never would have hit bottom and realized the path I was going down. Without you, I never would have learned how to survive on nothing. Without you, I never would have learned to appreciate the nice things.

This book is dedicated to my suicide attempt. Without you, I would not have been shown the protecting hand of God, that showed me I was meant for a bigger, better purpose.

This book is dedicated to Brooke, who believed in me in my darkest hours and sacrificed her own life to wake me up from a life that was not aligned with my purpose.

Resources

On the Web:

Aaron Nash – Coach

www.RealPlatinumFitness.com

Locations:

Platinum Fitness College Parkway

8595 College Pkway., Unit 190
Fort Myers, Florida 33919

(239) 839-8749

Platinum Fitness Cape Coral

2612 Santa Barbara Blvd.
Cape Coral, Florida 33914

(239) 823-7282

Platinum Fitness Gulf Coast

9961 Interstate Commerce Drive, Suite 100
Fort Myers, Florida 33913

(239) 839-7365

The Darkside Dichotomy

Unleashing Your True Power Through Pain

By Aaron Nash

Table of Contents

Foreword 1

Introduction 3

Chapter 1: Pain is Leverage 9

Chapter 2: Your Addictive Mindset is an Asset 23

Chapter 3: The Ingredients to Insane Success 37

Chapter 4: Customize Your Plan for Permanent & Positive Change 47

Chapter 5: Stop Comparing Yourself to Your Competition 63

Chapter 6: Getting Right With Your Ego 75

Chapter 7: Giving Back Leads to Abundance 93

Chapter 8: The One Surefire Way to Get Un-Stuck 103

Chapter 9: Accepting Help is a Superpower 117

Chapter 10: Being True to Yourself 127

Chapter 11: Put Your Darkness to Work 139

Acknowledgments 151

About the Author 153

Foreword

I was honored when Aaron asked me to write the first page you'll read before diving into his book. That's a lot of responsibility if you think about it. After all, a guy puts his life's work into consumable content in the form of a book, and he trusts me enough to make a hell of a first impression?!

That's pretty cool.

The day I met Aaron, I was inside the ballroom of the Ritz Carlton in Laguna Nigel, California, when my friend Bedros Keuilian was on stage speaking to the audience. In the middle of one of his sentences, he looked to the right side of the room and said, "Stewman, great to see you in here, man!"

But I was sitting on the *left side* of the room...

Bedros thought Aaron was me.

From that moment, the joke was on. Everyone now knows I'm officially a better-looking version of Aaron! I mean, the gag never gets old.

One night in St Louis, I pulled up to the Four Seasons and thought I saw Aaron walking in. I yelled out the Uber window, "Is that Ryan Stewman?" and the guy wasn't Aaron. What's funnier is the guy knew me and was like, "Did you just announce yourself?" We both cracked up.

It's because of these instances that I've created a great bond and friendship with Aaron. We met through a network we both belong to called Arete. It's filled with exclusive, high-level folks who must invest money to be a member.

Aaron and I have spent a lot of time together in person and online over the last year. And I can tell you, Aaron is on a mission. He's the type of person who when he says he's going to do something; he fucking means it. To be where he is in life after going through the shit you'll read about, is no miracle; it's the manifestation of hard work, grit and a don't-look-back mindset.

Aaron is building an empire that helps people live a better life. People he does business with go on to live their best lives. They beat obesity, regain their competitive edge, overcome diabetes, and more. He's truly doing sainted work in the form of owning a gym franchise.

Aaron is an amazing father, husband and friend. If I know one thing about him, he's loyal to his family of choice. You'll read all about his loyalty—even to a fault a few times—in this book.

Lastly, I want to give you a fair warning. After you read this book, you can't go back to living a life of excuses without admitting you are giving up. This book shows you what's possible through the eyes of Aaron Nash, but what you see through your eyes can tell a similar story in a few years—if you just learn the lessons he's shared and implement them.

Don't just read this book. *Live* what you learn. That's what will separate you from the rest of the pack.

Enjoy,

Ryan Stewman
CEO PhoneSites
Sign up for a Free Trial today PhoneSites.com/Closer

Introduction

This book shares the truth of a few. It contains the opposite of what most other books out there are talking about, the opposite of what you hear in videos and read on social media.

This book is about the truth of darkness.

And the truth is that you have demons inside you.

The truth is that you are flawed.

The truth is...

We all have a dark side; we have pain; we have negative emotions; we pop off excuses as to why we aren't achieving.

We all hold hate, ego, comparison, addiction, jealousy, ange, and depression inside us. We all cave into vices and other negative attractions in our lives.

But what you are about to read is what will give you the edge over other people who don't know how to use darkness to leverage their best lives. This secret is what will allow you to survive. It is the secret of what separates the winners from the losers...

The Dark Secret

Unbridled power lies coiled up in darkness. It is being used inside you right now, so the question you need to ask yourself is this...

Am I letting the power of my dark side stop me from achieving greatness, or am I letting it propel me to greatness?

Let's get real about what we've done wrong so we can make it right. Let's make sure we are 100% honest when we answer these questions, too—and there will be many throughout this book.

Through your honest answers and the potency of darkness, you will get much farther down your path than you have gotten for years.

You cheated?

You're addicted to drugs?

You came from a broken home?

You've had everything taken from you?

You didn't have a place to live for a week because you were a shit human to all your friends?

You've been lied to?

You've lost the girl you were dating on her way to take you out for your birthday because she was texting you and driving?

You have fucked up life so badly you couldn't even figure out how to kill yourself successfully?

Me too.

But here is the truth...

You can create a list like the one I just rattled off above so people will pity you. And I promise they will feel bad for your struggles. But the reason they will feel bad is that they know if your life is shit, you won't outshine them. That makes them feel bad for you but also relieved for themselves. After all, they are shining brighter!

You can look at the above list and think you don't deserve the gifts God has given you through these struggles. I could do the same thing.

You can worry about what other people will say or do. I could, too, but I don't.

I know that 99% of you reading this will care what other people think about you. I want you to start working on not giving a shit about that right now.

Even though this book will show you the truth and lessons that derive directly from the dark side, it's easier to live in ignorance.

It's easier to be shit.

It's easier to focus on that list, which means...

It's easier to live below what you are capable of doing and just be "good enough" because you fucked up your chance.

Fuck thinking like that.

Instead, ask yourself what lessons come from my pain?

I asked myself: did I actually fail at killing myself, or did God know that I was meant for greatness, and he wasn't done with me yet?

When you can ask yourself these types of questions about your pain and darkness, that's true power.

Don't believe me?

Reflecting Darkness

Look in the mirror. Ask yourself the most brutal question you can think of, that holds the answer you are the most afraid of.

Then watch your eyes as you answer yourself. Now, try to tell me your eyes don't tell you the truth...of what you already know.

What emotion reflected back at you?

Sadness?
Shame?
Anger?

Sometimes pain comes with anger, and it's hard to get rid of anger, especially if this is who we identify as being—the pissed human.

Sometimes, pain brings shame.

And sometimes, pain morphs into sadness.

Now, if you really want to change and make your life a million fucking times better, ask yourself one or all of the questions below as you stare yourself down in the mirror:

Did you lose everything growing up to spite you, or to teach you gratitude for the little things? To teach you that you can survive on much less than you think? BTW, the ability to function on next to nothing is a superpower.

Did you cheat on your wife because you are a piece of shit and don't deserve love? Or can you use this mistake to realize the power in truly having a teammate? In truly having a woman who will fight with you for the life you both want? Imagine that ride or die next to you! How untouchable would you be?

Did someone call you on some shit you aren't proud of? Cool! Do you realize when people point out your flaws, and you work on fixing them, that you become invincible? People who hate give you the power to fix your weaknesses.

Throughout this book, you'll learn that I am right there with you, working hard on what I want to improve in my life despite my wins.

You are going to get triggered reading this book, and when you do, I want you to remember two facts:

1) I wrote this book for me first, then I wrote it for you. Because if I can write down my struggles and realize them, I can be aware of them. That means I can change what I know if I have a plan and act on it. You, too!

2) You are more powerful than anyone around you. You aren't a mutant. You aren't broken. That feeling twisting up your gut is your potential screaming at you. This is your opportunity to tap into the dark side to achieve anything you want.

So, let's do it together. Step-by-step. Chapter by chapter. Then let's keep going and take another step, and another one after that. Let's do everything we can do to be perfect in the moment. Let's do everything we can to be honest so we can rise above everything trying to suppress us.

I'm ready. Are you?

Here we go!

Chapter 1: Pain is Leverage

Aaron Nash

✱✱✱

What if I told you there is no such thing as ignoring pain? What if I told you pain is being unleashed in your life, and you only have two choices when that happens...you can either let the pain make you a victim, or you can use the pain to guide you to your best self.

Your pain is being used right now, as you embark on this journey. And you can decide to either destroy or unleash your potential through it. If you are letting anger, jealousy, hate, ego, competition, scarcity, depression, anxiety, or any other emotion paralyze you from your potential, then keep reading. You need to!

Your pain is not going to go anywhere unless you move it out of the way. It is not something that can be numbed or ignored. In short...

You are in charge of the agony and ecstasy in your life.

You are also the boss when it comes to the level of physical or emotional pain you will feel.

Pain is like darkness to many people. Most people expect they will have a negative experience with pain. When we have that expectation, we get so fixated on having a bad experience that we forget there is a gift in pain. We forget pain is the best teacher.

Pain Can Teach Us

We can use it to learn not to race into the street as kids.

We can use it to learn not to re-engage with a train-wreck ex.

We can use it as motivation to complete a job.

We can channel it into energy.

We can decide how we will receive it in our bodies. Are we going to let it mangle us, or are we going to draw motivation from it?

Not everything about pain is bad.

Many times, people who hit rock bottom find their way up—because there is no other direction to go.

Pain does that.

Pain leads to major changes in our lives where we wouldn't have moved forward otherwise.

Pain is even positive. When you feel something wrong in your body, you know you need help. When you get help, you get better.

It is far easier to dwell on the physical and mental pain you feel than to do the inner work of pushing past it. Anyone can dwell on the pulsing hell of pain, reliving tragedy over and over again until they die. It takes massive intention, focus, and determination to rise above pain. That does not mean pain will go away, and this book is designed to teach you that we don't want it to because pain can be the defining factor in discovering our purpose. Pain can help us dig deep enough to discover the power in our purpose.

We are conditioned to brace ourselves when we feel pain, or even if we feel that pain is looming. Think about the last time you knew you were going to break up with a significant other. Did you brace yourself to feel that pain?

Of course, you did because when we know pain is coming, it's impossible to ignore it. This is a basic defense mechanism we use to protect ourselves.

Since it's hammered into our heads to try to survive pain, versus see the good that can come from it, it makes sense that asking you to view pain through a different lens feels weird.

But trust me on this. If you want to change your reaction to pain, you have to challenge yourself. You have to condition yourself to react to it in the opposite way of how you would normally react.

As you teach yourself to see pain differently, cut yourself a break, FFS. Remember, you are retraining your brain, and you will fuck up and not nail this whole "look at pain with a different perspective" thing. You won't go from zero to 100% the first time you try to switch up your response to pain. You might only nail your new plan once and then skip it twice, then nail it four times, and slip up the fifth. That's okay because you're still making more progress than before.

If we can't move away from the negative interpretation of pain, we will get stuck in it.

This means we have to do the work to improve our lives.

We are *always going to have pain in our lives. You can't escape that.*

Most people don't do the work. They have no idea how to change or even what to do to change.

This is why, in my opinion, you will see people unable to budge from horrible events in their lives for decades. They might experience the death of someone close to them, or been homeless, or fired, for example, but the difference between the people who triumph over their pain and those who stay stuck is mindset.

When you are stuck in pain, it is miserable, and you and I both know that many people are unable to handle their pain without a little help from an addictive substance or habit. Sure, drugs, alcohol, or even sex might help you wrestle that pain down. I used addiction to distract me and bury my pain because I couldn't face it head-on without something to take off that razor edge that felt like it would kill me—I hurt so badly.

The sooner you can confront your pain and create a plan to handle it, the more likely you are to move through your most challenging life events.

I sank into sex, drugs, and alcohol addiction for over a decade after my dad left.

When he came out of the closet after all-nighters at the bars, only to come home and kick my mom out of their room, it hurt. When we found out our longtime "family friend" was my dad's lover, it hurt. When everyone in school found out he tried to molest my best friends; it hurt so fucking bad.

When a girl I had been dating for a bit, Brooke, died. It didn't just hurt; I was shocked I hadn't died.

I sent Brooke the last text she read right before she hit a tree. On my birthday. On her way to take me out for the night. At the time, I was still coming out of drug addiction, so everything was about me. All of a sudden, I couldn't reach her. She wasn't picking up the phone, and I made that about me. I was pissed at her for standing me up. I was pissed she wasn't answering. It never even crossed my mind that something might be wrong.

The next day at work, my friend Kyle called me, not knowing Brooke and I had reconnected after a brief break from seeing each other. He told me she had hit a tree and died.

I missed her so intensely, with no idea what to do to feel better.

Of course, I had the worst kind of pain there is...the kind that comes from being responsible for someone else losing their life. (Or, so I thought).

This pain eviscerated every part of me. I had killed Brooke in my mind.

I had to punish myself.

I didn't think I deserved to live after that, so I tried to take myself out of this world by finding as much coke to take as possible. To add more hell to my agony, I hit the bottle as hard as I could and then deliberately rammed my car into the back of a horse trailer. I was out of my mind but could still reason that if I missed the trailer because I was so piss-wasted that the trees lining the road would kill me off. By some miracle, I didn't die. The car was totaled, and I didn't even have a bruise to show for my brilliant plan. I was high on drugs and the cop who pulled me over let me go after hearing about Brooke and how she died. He said I had suffered enough and took me back to the station until my mom could pick me up. You want to know how low you feel when you are such a fuck-up that you can't even successfully kill yourself?

Ask me.

When I woke up the next day, I realized how insanely lucky I was and that God had a plan for me. He spared me from that horse trailer and those trees. He spared me from an easy 3-5 years in the slammer and the downward spiral that would have eventually killed me like any drug.

That was the first time I felt I needed to be more.

Shortly after that, I got into the mindset that I needed to kick my addictions permanently. Even deciding that made me see my life differently. I viewed the obstacles in my path as opportunities instead of hardships. I identified areas where I could grow and where I could help other people grow.

I knew if Brooke had lived out her life to her fullest potential, she would have gone on to help others. Since she can't do that, I am picking up where she left off... I am on a mission to change people's lives, to help make them better and healthier and happier in the world. The pain that ravaged me when I learned she was gone can't be wasted...otherwise, what is the point of her life? What would be the point of mine?

If I had taken the path of not giving a shit, two lives would've been lost.

That epiphany that I *should* go on, that it was *okay* to go on gave me a new focus on life. I was so happy and relieved to have a reason to obsess over solutions, not problems. And it wasn't that I wasn't still grieving—because of course, I was, but grieving eventually fades until you can live with the pain. I had to do the mental work to convince myself that *yes, while we were texting, I was not solely responsible for the accident.* I couldn't punish myself over and over again. More importantly, I didn't want to.

Because of everything I have been through, I have learned:

You don't have to be in hell to rise up. You don't have to cause or struggle with adversity in your life so you can overcome it.

I know this is hitting home if you are a person who self-sabotages. If you are a miserable SOB lurking in the blackness of your own life.

Does any of this sound familiar?

Do you set out on better paths only to get nervous when you feel your life changing significantly? Then do you make choices to burn your progress? Do you destroy what you have worked so hard to build?

Pain is not a required ingredient in success. You can actually make good and healthy decisions that lead you to be your best self as your demons snap at your heels and push you *toward* the light.

As nuts as it sounds, you can just GO INTO the light.

You can just climb the ladder without drama.

After having gone through the pain I have, I don't want you to suffer.

But what did I mean when I said that you are in charge of your own agony or ecstasy?

I meant this...

Pain is Subjective

Everyone experiences pain differently and reacts to it in different ways.

If what you have gone through had affected someone else, would you advise them to respond to their pain the way you did? With hindsight, a lot of us might answer differently.

A lot of us wouldn't choose to handle our pain the same...knowing that rejecting the darkness of pain caused greater misery. Knowing that waiting to feel better and be better, meant we were wasting time.

The truth is, everyone has their shit. Every story is full of ups and downs. My drug addiction was easy to explain to people. I was pitied for having to go through that rough patch when my dad left us broke and alone with nothing. Many people believe that statistics show not many people who grow up in a broken home and are drug addicts end up succeeding at any level, but here is the biggest lie you have been told... The statistics actually say regardless of what you have been through or where you came from, your odds at creating true success are incredibly low; that's why they call it the 1%. So, for those of you using your pain as pity, now you're fucked. Your level of pain has nothing to do with your chances of achieving success.

Go back and read that again. Once you realize it doesn't matter what you have been through, and all that matters is your response, you may just have your eyes opened to the truth.

It's a tough fucking truth, and I never promised you an easy read!

This is why the one-upping of our pain needs to stop.

Just because someone else doesn't seem to be experiencing the same level of pain you are, doesn't mean they aren't. Stop the pain comparisons already.

Everyone receives pain differently, and we are all wired in individual ways. In fact, even if the same circumstances applied to both of us, we would still receive the experience differently. Maybe a friend or relative had a recent setback that seemed minor to you, but you wondered why the hell they were overreacting. The truth about that situation is that your friend or family member may be overwhelmed by what has happened. They may feel what happened more deeply and intensely than you would've. It might affect areas of their life where the same areas in your life would be barely touched.

We can't standardize our responses to pain.

And we shouldn't try.

No one's pain is more or less. It is also helpful to remember that another person's pain is not about you...unless you slam their toes in the door or tell them their haircut sucks.

But how in the world do you even begin to approach navigating pain positively? We have to have a place to start...especially when we have been conditioned to reject pain.

I asked myself one simple question when I was trying to view pain positively, and I think it will help you, too. Ask yourself: *What are the powers of this pain?* You don't understand what you are capable of when you use your pain.

Remember pain gives you an extra gear you can engage to your benefit. This gear sits there when you don't need it, and some of us forget its existence when life is going along well. This pain, this gear is a tool that allows your bandwidth for pain to widen. You can take on more.

Let this pain gear kick your instincts into action and protect you.

We can't compare how we think we might respond or hold up to pain to how we really will respond when we are in the thick of intense and unrelenting pain. The cool thing about the pain gear is, the more you realize it is there, and the more you shift into it, the more you begin to understand that you are one powerful motherfucker capable of anything.

You are capable of beating anything. You are capable of turning on the light out of pitch-black pain.

Addiction and the inability to face the truth of your life are huge red flags that you are wallowing in pain. That you aren't using the pain, instead the pain is using you.

Deaths can last decades. Losses can stretch to forever when they haunt you...because you breathe life into them over and over again.

My healing began in the gym.

Every time I worked out, I felt good. Since the age of 14, the gym has lit me up. Going back and rediscovering my purpose and how good I felt made me want to recreate that reality for myself more and more. That's not to say that I didn't give in to every single one of my emotions when I was in the pits of hell. I did. I was depressed. I couldn't give a shit less about anything in my life. But I still went to the fucking gym.

The gym was working its magic. It was bringing me back to life.

One day, after I first started training other people in the gym with my childhood friend, I went home and told my mom, "This is what my life needs. I found it."

The cold metal of the 200-pound weights didn't care how I felt. If I was happy, sad, suicidal, whatever my mood, 200 pounds was 200 pounds, no matter what was going on in my head.

The side effects of choosing power over pain trickled in. After I opened my gym, I worked with people whose transformations were mind-blowing. People who had been overweight and spent most of their lives hating themselves stripped away all that self-resentment and disappointment along with the weight. These people hugged me as tears streamed down their faces.

When they did everything they could to be their best selves, they saw their potential, and it broke them in the best way. It broke their dusty, old opinions of themselves. It shattered their poor self-esteem. It murdered their doubts.

These people that I was training never dreamed they could enjoy their lives or that they wouldn't always loathe themselves.

Yes, the gym was taking me to an even better place than I imagined, but I wasn't done fucking around yet.

I told you bad habits are hard to break, and pain is a bitch to walk away from

Even after all the dumb shit I did, I was only thrown in jail once. One day that changed. I got a DUI and had to sleep in a jail cell overnight. The way I was living my life, it's a small miracle I never spent more time behind bars. But once my direction became clear, all of a sudden, it hit me.

I had been spared so I could help other people learn to love themselves.

Challenge accepted.

I got lucky.

You have an edge over my luck as you sit there with this book in your hands. You can make a choice to be good to yourself instead of praying to ride out your shitty decisions.

And this is a note to my fellow fitness peeps before I close out this chapter: I don't care what section of the fitness world you work in. We are in the business of training people to finally love themselves as they become their healthiest. We are responsible for training their minds to become healthier, so they stop justifying their harmful behavior. Over the last five years, I have become ultra-successful because I am in alignment with what I am supposed to do. It is incredible when all the elements of your life click into place, and you can suddenly see the road ahead. I want you to have that feeling, too. I want to be there for you every step of the way as you shed damaging beliefs about yourself and your potential. As you leave pain in the dust.

Ask yourself these questions that I used to pull myself out of a depression years ago.

Write them down so you will stare them in the face and can't hide from the work you need to do to move forward.

1. What caused your pain?

2. What are you doing about it?

3. Are you self-medicating to numb the pain?

4. Do you avoid talking about this pain?

5. What could your pain be poured into, and how could it fuel your progress?

Chapter 2: Your Addictive Mindset is an Asset

Aaron Nash

***

More and more addictions are poking their heads up from underground than ever before. These are foods and habits we had never considered addictions. But they have just as much potential to control your life even if they don't seem hardcore.

Today we know these addictions are actually harmful:

Sugar
Fast food
Soda
Chocolate
Coffee

That's the mild list.

Of course, we've all heard about the super-intense life-crashing addictions:

Drugs
Smoking
Drinking
Sex
Gambling
Stealing
Lying
And the list goes on...

Power in Destruction

We cling to addictions because they are distracting, fulfilling, justifying, rewarding, and they give us negative attention. Sometimes, we like to receive negative attention because it beats not having any attention at all, and we don't know how to get positive attention. As a human being, any kind of attention feels good, even the wrong kind.

Despite the downfalls of addiction, there is one positive aspect. Having an addictive personality can be one of your best personality traits. Think of it this way...if you can get so distracted by smoking or drinking, you can also turn your personality into what can be good for you.

Sure, it sucks ass to feel like you are in the grip of something you can't control. But there is more to your addiction and bad habits. If you ignore the power within destruction, you are robbing yourself. You are not even letting yourself learn how fucking focused you can be.

Just as you can become obsessed with destruction, so, too, can you become obsessed with production.

People with addictive personalities have a ridiculous ability to concentrate. They are wired to fixate, and when they flip the script from fixating on what will destroy them, to what will build them...they learn they are unstoppable.

Let me ask you: *do you think anyone out there who has attained massive success did it half-ass?*

Of course, not!

Colossal success REQUIRES insane fixation on your goal.

Let's say you want to reach for the booger sugar, for instance. You can't think of anything else. You want that drug so badly you can feel it in your body, what it does to you. You sink into the sensations it causes.

You can go just as hard on *anything* else. You can grind yourself into the ground growing your business once you kick drugs.

And it is possible to beat addictions; I don't want to split hairs with you on this topic. Yes, it's hard to quit, but you can do it. Keep in mind when life gets hard, and you feel alone or abandoned, you will trigger hard and may want to start up again.

That's why I've labeled this next section, "Addiction Triggers." Because I want you to understand why you might be more likely to fall off the wagon, and even why you picked up a terrible habit in the first place. Do you think you would ever pick up a glass, a smoke, a blunt, or whatever else you might use to deaden your pain if your life had been perfect and without pain?

Probably not.

Addiction Triggers:

1. **Anger/frustration** – I struggle with this emotion the most. It's so easy to go right to anger and frustration as the answer to trying situations. When people piss me off, I have to get into my head and take a step back. My first reaction is to say, "Fuck you!" but I know this is not always the right response. (FYI: it's not always the wrong one either—anger can be useful and give you the courage to set boundaries, for example). But anger can turn into a one-night stand, a hit, a drink, a card game, whatever you want to use. Which...can become an addiction.

2. **Trauma** – You know those snapshot moments that split your life into before and after? Before your brother died, you were *this* person, and now that he is gone, you are *that* person. We know after trauma, we will never be the same. We will never, no matter what we do, be able to bring back someone who died. We will never be able to undo abuse. We will never be able to not feel the weight of rejection. We will never forget what it means to feel like we aren't good enough. This even applies to your economic status. We get caught up in the comparison game. *I am always going to be poor. I am always going to be abused. I am never going to find another love again.* Then sometimes, to pour a little more salt in our gaping wounds, we add *I don't deserve to recover from this pain or to have what other "normal" people do.* Trauma is a liar, just like depression and anxiety. We can certainly understand what is attractive about high-tailing it from this pain.

3. **Diagnosis** – "You have a 20 percent chance of surviving this aneurysm before we operate." *Great, I'll spend most of my time blitzed.* "Mom," your 15-year-old announces, "I'm pregnant." *The right thing to do feels like it might be: I need to stuff ALL the sugar and garbage I can in my face. I need to feel some sort of security, dammit.* Of course, we know that is a load of shit!

4. **Relationships** – *Stop the shitty merry-go-round, I want to get off.* Sound familiar? Relationships are challenging, and the good ones are terrifying because they force you to half-Nelson yourself into confronting all the things you need to work on. Relationships can be the worst mirror, especially if we never had a happy and healthy dynamic modeled for us. Then it's a crapshoot, more like: *I guess this is what it looks like to have a long-term relationship.* Navigating the feelings, and the shock of how human your partner can be and yes, even worrying

about too much routine, can lead a person to skip doing the work to build the foundation needed for a relationship to survive. And then...they might dive straight to the bottom of a glass.

Rocky relationships can be a root of substance abuse, and that abuse can also trigger hard times. How much do we scold ourselves for not knowing better than to do something or say something that hurt the people we give a shit about when we were *never taught* how to have relationships? Sometimes, we are so cruel to ourselves.

Relationships reveal all, and they also have the potential to give us the love and even the families we have always wanted. Tell me that isn't some scary ass shit. Relationships have everything to do with practice and conditioning, too. You learn to stop freaking out at every minor argument. You learn when is the right time to table a discussion because you don't want to say the wrong thing. But sometimes, what you want so badly scares the shit out of you so much, that using allows the pain to be livable.

5. **Conflict** - Personal, business, any sort of conflict. If you hate conflict if you assign it more depth and meaning than the situation calls for, it might feel good to pour out a couple of fingers or hit the pipe. It might feel good to literally bury yourself in a new chick too often. But what you are doing is entombing the pain when you do this. You are becoming a master distractor.

Family, lovers, children, work, bosses, just being in public. Life is filled with conflict potential, but it doesn't have to make you come undone.

6. **Self-love or lack thereof** – It's okay to admit to yourself that you weigh more than you want, and I even advise

my clients to use the "F" word: fat. Don't run from the truth or allow yourself to be insulted by the power you assign words. If you are fat, stop the habit that made you that way, and that continues to make you fatter.

No changes can be made unless you accept the truth of where you are at—whether that is where you want to be or not. If you say you are these things, you become the source and the starting point. *I am making myself this way* is a helpful self-statement and forces you to do something about the truth you uncover. Self-loathing thrives on body image issues.

Choosing every day to stay at a job you can't stand is another example of self-loathing. We hate ourselves in all kinds of ways, and when you hate yourself, you don't care if you punish yourself. You probably think you have it coming. It takes tremendous willpower to turn self-hatred around and assessing the road that needs to be walked, that HAS to be walked to get to the best version of you makes many people choose the easier path…addiction, laziness, settling.

You've got to come to the realization that you deserve more than self-sabotaging your life. If you want to get out of these cycles, look for the light in the dark.

I told you, it's fucking there!

Addiction Feels Like Control

Even an out-of-control, bottom-of-the-gutter addiction makes us feel *in control*.

We know every fact about our addiction because we are so busy defending it.

I only allow myself one pack of cigarettes every three days. I'm in control.

We love to fuck with the details of addiction, too. The cool shot glasses or bongs or other toys. We love to play with shit because it is the best distraction in the world against pain.

We figure people still care about us even as they are harping on us to quit and certainly when they don't have the spine or balls to tell us that we are terrifying them.

Harping on us = loved ones don't want us to die.
Not harping on us = loved ones are just waiting for us to figure out our shit.

Deep inside, we know the truth. We know that what we are doing is so destructive that we are stripping away all our potential because what if we try to stop and fail? At least when we are using, we can lie and say that *we know we can quit whenever we want...* Isn't it so comforting to live with what seems like a harmless lie?

And what happens to the pain when we take away our crutch?

When we put the bottle down, and everything comes roaring back like a pain avalanche crashing on us, suffocating us, what do we do then?

How are we supposed to live with the pain that we have repressed and turned from a mouse into a demon who will rip out your god-damned throat?

So, of course, addictions are like an anesthetic.

We might even think they allow us to function, to work, be a better parent, lover, dog owner, whatever.

Here's a secret that every addict knows...they get that their fucked-up life doesn't match others.

Does it make sense for the college student to drink by themselves?

Does it make sense to only get high or drunk after work?

Does it make sense to try heroin just one more time, and *then I'll be done*?

That is some fucked-up reasoning, and you know it. Every addict knows it, too, and because they do, it compounds their original pain. More and more pain piles up on the addiction.

You *know* when your life is off the rails, and you're deep-down *not happy* about it, but the pain of what waits for you on the other side without your numbing agent is greater than you think you can bear.

So, it goes. This is the cycle of addiction.

This is you circling the drain and being terrified that you are the only lifeguard in this scenario.

But what if one day that lifeguard shows up so trashed they can't save you?

Meaning, you can't save you? Well, you'll live with that, too and maybe if you're extra nice to yourself you might even suggest that *hey, you're a piece of shit anyway, so you kinda deserve to die.*

Overcoming Your Addictions

If you see yourself here and you hate this chapter, good.

It means a part of you is still in there who wants to be better more than you want to be sick.

You are over the excuses you give yourself.

You are, as the saying goes, becoming one of these people on the verge of major improvement who first MUST get tired of their own shit.

I like to think of it a different way: that you can't take any more pain.

But how do you stop?

The one thing all former addicts have in common is that when they quit for good, they didn't allow any excuses.

You know what I mean…

I'll see how quitting goes and hope that I can do it.

You better say out loud and MEAN IT that you WILL do it.

You better say: *I can quit. Period. I will quit—end of story.*

If you are not in this frame of mind, you are not ready to quit.

What's the difference between people who reach their goals and those who don't?

It's simple.

Perseverance.

Every single winner has that in common.

The lightweight champion of the world conditions his body and mind every day.

Billionaire magnates do what they have to do to remain in the top percent of earners in the world.

A goal achieved by dumb luck has a very low chance of being achieved again.

You know how you get lucky on the driving range sometimes, and every element of you connects with the ball? You didn't send that ball into the stratosphere because you KNEW what to do. You didn't plan that swing. You tried, but it was dumb luck that you hit it just right. If you were to hit it again, you would likely not be able to repeat the shot.

In overcoming addiction, you have to figure out what works. How to hit the shot every time without fail. There's no more relying on luck.

Addiction recovery is not one and done. That's the first step. The second step is living your conviction to stay clean and sober every waking minute of your life.

Adjust the focus of the fire of your addictive personality. Get hyper-focused on something else that is good for you.

Remember, what got you into trouble can keep you out.

Thinking of recovery this way always made me feel better.

As much as I was a maniac about using drugs and sex, I am as much a maniac today when it comes to taking care of my body.

All you are doing is tipping the pendulum to the other side.

And…if you have an intense and driven-AF personality you KNOW you will go through life always feeding that hunger. It's like being on the island on *Naked and Afraid* where you are forced to hunt to live.

What compels you doesn't have to kill you. It can actually PROPEL you. That can be enough.

It's pretty amazing if you think about it.

The power that you have.

To make a different decision at any time.

To live a different life.

To flip a switch inside and actually give a shit about yourself.

You just need to tap into it.

If the fear of making the change has you second-guessing what you need to do, for now, don't worry about eradicating the fear. Let your heart race, your stomach churn, and your face get hot, then accomplish what you want to do ANYWAY.

Aaron Nash

Chapter 3: The Ingredients to Insane Success

***

Do you know why most resolutions fail?

Would you guess it's because people don't try hard enough, or because they try too hard?

Sounds weird, but the answer is actually that people who want to change try too hard in the beginning. They go at their goal with every resource they have, and they burn out!

This is why you see the gyms bursting to max capacity in January.

It's why the first two or three days of a drastic new diet stick.

People want too much from themselves, and they set the bar way too high. They are ready to nearly kill themselves to prove *I can do it. I am a badass. I am finally changing despite what anyone else said.*

Go Small or Go Home

Here's another fact: the smallest changes can make the biggest differences.

Instead of envisioning the finish line after a monster marathon, try one of these visions instead:

- You, drinking four more glasses of water tomorrow.
- You, parking in the farthest possible spot away from work

- You, switching out your mid-day candy bar for pre-cut fruit chunks.
- You, taking the stairs instead of the elevator.
- You, meditating for 10 minutes at night instead of Facebooking.

The point is, there are small habit and mindset shifts you can make every day. And, if you fall off the wagon, remember what determines a successful trajectory is not a perfect track record.

What determines success is the person who keeps trying no matter if they fall down. No matter how many times they fall down...

This is why mindset is so critical to succeeding. That means honing your self-talk. It means conditioning your mind to reach your goals as often as possible. You need to get into the habit of pepping yourself up if you stumble. That moment of vulnerability is telling. How will you get back to it? This isn't the time to justify a slip. You know what I'm talking about; *well, fuck it. I screwed up so I might as well eat this box of cookies.* When you are in that headspace what does that type of justification do for you? It's relieving, isn't it? It's you saying *I don't have to try as hard anymore. I knew I would fail, so I might as well accept my weaknesses.*

Doing the work and staying on track is hard. It might sound incredibly simple, but the easiest way to attain what you want is to learn to channel your emotions. You can also train yourself to shut them off. Because there is a time for getting in your head and a time for focusing on your progress.

We mess ourselves up because:

- We get tired and want to give in.
- We overthink our potential.
- We are afraid to let go of what is familiar…even if the familiar sucks.
- We compare ourselves to other people we admire, but we often forget that they have been at the game for far longer than we have.
- We get resentful at the pain change brings.
- We don't realize how vital mental reinforcement is.

When you set out to improve your life, think about making a minor shift consistently.

Drink lemon water for lunch today. Just count on doing this today. Don't think about how you will feel after consuming 365 bottles of lemon water. Think about the determination it takes to reach for the water and add the lemon. That's it! It doesn't sound like much does it? I'm sure you are thinking *well, that's a snap! I could do that without any issues at all.* Awesome! That means you're getting it!

Now, it's time to implement the second step. Do it tomorrow and the day after tomorrow and the day after that and that and that and that. When you think about it this way, those actions add up, don't they?

When we are on the outside looking in at someone else's goal-getting, we only see the actions that person is taking. We aren't in their heads checking out their thoughts. We don't hear what they tell themselves when they have a bad day. We don't hear how they struggle to remain nice to themselves if they make a mistake. When you get into the habit of talking down to yourself, and you want to improve that, it won't happen overnight.

Newsflash: Abso-fucking-lutely nothing worth having happens overnight.

Commit to Committing

Let's say you are a person who comes from a stressful family situation where the people around you are pretty toxic. I don't care who it is either...we could be talking about your mom, dad, sister, brother, grandparents, and even the person you might consider your BFF. We align with people in our lives initially due to proximity (family and school friends—they are physically close by) and because we can relate to each other.

If you had a poor upbringing and weren't shown a lot of love and attention, you get used to that kind of treatment. It's not shocking to be around people who have a defeatist attitude and who are even abusive. But you cannot EVER achieve the highest level of yourself if you are not surrounded by people who push themselves to be the best.

Switching to a positive mindset after having exactly the opposite drilled into you for years and finding that new faith in yourself is going to be HARD.

You are going to have to commit to committing to believing in yourself.

To do this, first, you need to warm up your mind, like a runner stretching and jogging in place before the race. Instead of allowing shit rivers to run through your thoughts, simply make the promise to yourself that *I will commit to committing.*

You will commit to committing to work out for 30 minutes a day, three times a week. That's it. Drive your ass to the gym. Commit to getting to the parking lot. Commit to getting in your car.

Deconstruct your goals into mini-goals.

Yes, interrupting your patterns spikes your adrenaline but a short-lived surge is not enough to sustain you long-term.

Excitement gives you fuel, but it won't stay for the long-haul.

Think of it as the difference between a car starting and running. You need the key to crank the engine, but you have to give it gas to move forward. Then you need to repeat the motion to keep on rolling down the road.

The other elephant in the room you might have noticed is that we are so hard on ourselves. This goes back to the section we covered on self-talk. Again, your mindset will not change for the better without you *believing* it can.

It's true that it is a matter of *just doing it*, but you also need to practice, practice, practice, and believe that YOU CAN DO ANYTHING!

You are the Source and the Solution

People don't like the truth that they are the source and solution to all of their problems.

They also hate when they try to change, that some people around them will do anything to keep them on their same, miserable level. People like this pull you back down because misery loves company; they don't want to feel like they are the only loser. We are all responsible for our levels of happiness and struggle. So don't let someone else influence you into *not changing*. When you level up, you are taking no bullshit, but you are also letting others know you are not falling for their shit.

Seeing you miserable is *all about them*. It's all about their misery that gives them attention and allows them to make excuses.

When you make such a massive fucking change in your life, you better be your loudest cheerleader. Because for damn sure, everyone else who hates themselves will try to drown out your voice with their discouragement.

You better be a cheerleader after 20 energy drinks.

The only person you can depend on to truly support your transformation is YOU.

You must practice living your transformation.

I'll say it louder: **THE ONLY PERSON YOU CAN DEPEND ON TO TRULY SUPPORT YOUR TRANSFORMATION IS YOU.**

Make yourself big enough to drown out all the distractions.

Small shifts mean moving away from what's familiar. Insist on the support of yourself—even if you are the only one who is supporting your changing.

So, be the only one out there making a positive difference and kill it. It will drive the haters wild, and that's an entertaining side effect.

Make Yourself a Priority

I like the plan of taking 30 minutes a day for yourself to make yourself a priority. This time is mandatory. You can't postpone it; you can't cancel it. Leave your problems at the door. Nothing else but you matters during this time. Use this time for whatever you want, meditation, a workout, reading, it doesn't matter. Work on not worrying about anything else. You will be astounded to see what happens when you use 30 minutes for yourself every day.

When we are stressed, we can think that we need to do life so differently. Part of the reason for this is because people only see the headlines of each other's lives instead of watching the documentary. We get the highlight reel when we look in on someone else's shit, but never the work, sacrifice, or sabotage. We compare our lives in terms of opposites. If we don't like the way our life is going, we think about who has the best life around us. They probably have more money, more time, a better relationship, closer ties to the important people in their life.

But you do not see the whole picture.

Remember, we see what's on the surface and what other people want us to see.

We develop our opinions on their lives based on incomplete information. Then we fill in the gaps with what we think is the truth. So, making a change to be happier, thinner, etc., seems like a huge undertaking. But a half an hour makes all the difference in the world because most of the time, what needs to change is our perception of how we are taking care of ourselves.

Do you have a clue how tightly wound up you are?

Ask yourself, and I know this sounds crazy…

Have you forgotten how to take a vacation?

Or…

Are you even freaked out at the idea of taking a vacation?

What about meditating? Does being alone with your thoughts terrifying you?

We get so good at putting work before ourselves, excuses before ourselves, comfort before ourselves, other people's happiness and priorities before ourselves.

One of my friends takes a seven-minute vacation every day in the summer to swing outside in the hammock. Seven minutes, lying down, swinging in the breeze, eyes opened and looking up at the treetops. Feeling the sun. Inhaling the fresh air. Listening to nature in the grass, the pond, the trees. Seven damn minutes makes her a renewed person. Reminds her she is important and worth taking a minute for!

So are you.

You are worth it all.

The blood, sweat, and tears of trying, the hurts-so-good pain, the emotional workout, the pride of finally putting yourself first, you are worth it.

Self-care isn't just about finding the time to do something you wouldn't normally do. Eating better. Moving more. Feeling more secure. Being positive. Challenging yourself. Growing. Refusing too much comfort in your life.

Ask yourself: what are the basic pieces of you? Health, relationships, your purpose, your connection to this world, your finances, your intelligence; it all needs to be challenged.

So you will keep improving your life.

Don't get it twisted. You cannot have the life you want without being the best support system for yourself along the way.

Chapter 4: Customize Your Plan for Permanent & Positive Change

Aaron Nash

✽✽✽

You've read a lot of heavy shit now.

Know this: good information, useful information, and even life-changing information mean zilch unless you put action behind them.

Think of those self-help books that are nothing but a poorly disguised memoir and a chance for people to blow their own horns. I don't want this book to be like that for you. I don't want you to get to the end of this book and think *what the fuck, Aaron? What am I supposed to do with your childhood memories to make my life better?*

I know my memories mean more to me than anyone else. Just like yours mean more to you. That's normal.

If you want to change, you have to get off the nostalgic kick and define your next steps toward making permanent inroads.

You have to be able to look the challenge of personal change in the face and know you are strong enough to alter your habits.

So many people are afraid of talking about lasting change. Jawing 'bout, *I'll just start here and see where it goes.*

I am so tired of that crap.

This is the chapter where it gets real. It gets painful because you have to get up off your ass. You have to confront yourself in the mirror and stop lying and justifying.

If you are not ready, stop fucking around and put this book down until you are prepared to read what I have to tell you.

Step one. Get out of the light and move into the pain.

You read that right. It's not a typo. MOVE INTO YOUR PAIN.

Walk toward what you want to walk away from. Be a firefighter. Run into the flames to save your life.

Now, wrap your head around the fact that pain is not going to kill you.

Those memories that slice you wide open cannot stop your heart.

They can't steal your breath.

But you CAN relive them until you pull out the lesson you need.

And...

You ARE STRONG ENOUGH and POWERFUL ENOUGH to do it.

You're still reading, aren't you? That means you want to be here and do this.

The Process

Our aim at the gym is making a two-percent improvement every single day.

Meaning, every day, I teach my clients to slave over themselves to be two percent better than they were the day before. I live this same rule myself. No exceptions.

We already discussed this in the book, and if you need a refresher, go back to that chapter. Otherwise, let's move on. It's time to answer the age-old question:

Q: How do I even get to two percent?
A: Fucking prioritize yourself.

You can't spend your life making excuses to take care of other shit that doesn't matter and not prioritizing yourself.

It's not selfish to take care of yourself—as long as you have balance.

Handling your shit doesn't mean neglecting the other areas and people in your life.

It's doesn't mean you are going to pulverize it at the gym and be a piece of shit father.

It doesn't mean you are going to kill it in business and ignore your wife.

Life is all about balance.

So, knock off the idea that taking care of yourself is some woo-woo bullshit, and recognize if you want to be great, you have to pay attention to what you need Every. Single. Day.

Now, that you've got that through your head—and you better pound it in there, or you can't move forward—let's jump right into YOUR PAIN.

Every Person's Pain is Different

Remember, as we talked about, every person's pain is different and is caused by different events in their lives, but the type of event doesn't dictate the depth of pain.

Here's another example: person one could have starving kids and feel absolutely miserable, worried, and beat themselves up and person two could have lost a childhood friend in a horrific accident and feel a similar level of pain.

I am not saying the pain of your kids starving isn't heavier. But to the person who has never experienced seeing their children suffer, yet who has *lost* an old friend, *the impact of the pain may be similar.*

We have to stop comparing our pain.

Period.

Remember...

We are not here to measure each other's pain.

You are responsible for your own pain anyway, not anyone else's.

The person who is morbidly obese and trying to lose 100+ pounds has unique pain.

The person who was abandoned multiple times in their life has unique pain.

The person who is sick and terrified they fucked up their life so badly that they will die has unique pain.

The person leaving an abusive relationship has unique pain.

Do you see the common thread in pain?

Everyone's pain is unique, and so, as the old saying goes: "We're all unique, so no one is." Pain is the same. Even though it is different.

The Biggest Challenge to Making Change

What do you think the hardest struggle is for people who are trying to make a change in their lives?

When I ask this question in a coaching session, a lot of people get a smirk on their face and blurt out what they think is the right answer. But they are wrong when they assume it is the struggle to repeat healthy actions every single day.

The biggest challenge for people who want to make their lives different is admitting their struggle. It's admitting, "They have a problem," to quote every addiction book ever published.

Why do we make it so hard to come to terms with the demons in our lives?

And yes, you read that part right, too…

WHY DO <u>WE</u> MAKE IT HARD?

What is at stake that we do everything we can to avoid the truth of ourselves?

Is it because we are scared of the work?

The commitment?

The self-loathing?

That we can't keep our promises to ourselves?

Maybe it's a little bit of all of those things.

But I think it's guilt.

Let's go down the rabbit hole of self-beatings. Do you say one or more of these phrases to yourself?

I shouldn't have done that...

How did I get so fat?

Why did I let it get this far?

Why didn't I stop myself?

Don't I give a shit about me?

If I don't give a shit about me, doesn't that mean when I try to change, I will have to face the fact that I am a piece of crap?

What if I am not strong enough to come back from the shit I put myself through?

What if I find out that I don't care about myself and I never will?

Here's the delicious truth:

The ingredient in every shit sandwich is pain.

People who get the shaft give the shaft. That's a variation on what softer coaches say: "Hurt people hurt people."

I share this with you because it's fucking true.

No matter what you want to change, you have to address the pain.

I work with a lot of women who even though they swear they want to be in shape, stop themselves from getting there. And they do this without even realizing it. Being fat means being invisible. Being invisible means being safe from men. From being abused, from being sexually assaulted. Even from the drama, a relationship can bring. When I see a person resisting the potential of being their best self, it pisses me off. I don't get pissed at them. But I get frustrated that they would let such a damaging mentality rule their life and health.

It's not unusual for women to get started on the right foot, and to be enthusiastic about getting healthier and look better! I love seeing women like this in their element. They are ready to kick ass and snatch their power back. They can't wait to stop being a victim. Seriously, it charges me up.

But then it happens. The excitement fades because the pressure of needing to do the work sets in. They haven't learned healthy ways to set boundaries or to view themselves and instead fool themselves into believing they will be okay as long as they keep doing what they are doing...no matter how bad it is for them.

They are so obsessed with seeing what they believe is the good of their habits—that they can't see the truth. They are breaking themselves down one day at a time. They are accepting a weaker version of themselves.

It's death by a thousand paper cuts, or in this case, death by a thousand neglectful moments.

How hard is it to go to the gym for the first time after telling yourself that you are not worth it every moment of your life?

It's excruciating.

In reference to the women I am talking about, they are using their pain as a hindrance instead of *letting pain propel them.*

In the case of women who have been assaulted, I can't begin to understand how traumatic that is. What I can do is speak from my experience of helping women to define their pain, so it doesn't control them anymore. Understand, I am not dismissing the pain of abuse. Of course, not, and if you think that, fuck you, btw. I am saying I can see the pain behind these women's eyes as clearly as if the abuse had JUST happened when it might have taken place 40 years ago! It destroys me to see a person hold themselves hostage over the pain they received and that they didn't even cause. *Why keep punishing themselves when they didn't create and don't deserve such unrelenting and unbearable agony?*

Even after abuse, trauma, or any life-altering event, we still hold the power to choose how we live our lives.

As I write this, it feels like this is an unpopular thing to say. Some people might read into my words and say that they mean I am victimizing the victim all over again.

NO! I am not dismissing pain. I am talking about harnessing the power of ourselves to overcome pain. I am telling you that you have the power. You always have.

We might not have control over what kind of treatment we receive—especially in the case of abuse—but we sure as fuck have a choice about the level of pain we allow in our lives.

Does moving on remove the pain like it never existed?

Nope. It's not all or nothing. It's not NO pain or ALL the pain.

It's living with the pain and using it as leverage to catapult ourselves out of a self-imposed nightmare.

We do ourselves a disservice when we think we can't conquer anything.

Of fucking course, we can.

And do you know how we do this?

We decide to do it.

Don't feel worthwhile because of your shit childhood?

Decide you are worthy.

Don't feel like taking the abuse anymore?

Decide you are done.

Don't feel like you are a good father?

Decide to be one.

The power of choice, especially as it comes out of the darkest parts of ourselves, is one of our rarely used superpowers.

Stop fucking yourself over and decide.

People wonder why I'm so intense.

I don't do bullshit.

I don't do excuses.

I don't begin to allow someone to tell me they can't.

When I hear the word "can't" all I can think is *you haven't figured it out yet.*

No matter how many layers down our pain goes, it can be released from us.

We have to learn what we have control over, and I don't want to hear the BS story that we have no control.

Yes, we have control—over who we tell ourselves we are. Over who we want to be.

That means you can gain control over *how you handle anything and everything.*

Read it again: YOU CAN GAIN CONTROL OVER HOW YOU HANDLE EVERYTHING AND EVERYTHING.

Some of the women I coach to help release their pain, to meet their darkness and emerge in power had let their assaulters imprison them for decades.

Decades of living in hell.

Decades of living without hope, just being numb and responding to life automatically…without any feeling.

Being a dead version of who they used to be, of who they could be.

This is not harnessing the power of darkness but allowing the darkness to capture you.

It's like being kidnapped without chains or bonds, and then your captor leaving the door wide open while you hunker in the dim light in the dungeon. Unrestrained…yet still imprisoned.

Because you chose to stay there.

Eliminate another's control over you, and you have no crutch.

Eliminate another's control over you, and you have no excuse.

Most importantly, eliminate another's control over you, and you are limitless.

Realize letting the control of another person go means you will not get attention for the pain they caused you anymore.

That's another kind of addiction you can allow yourself to fall prey to—pity, drama, self-imposed chaos.

Is that really what you want to focus on—getting negative attention—when your life can be so much better?

So much more rewarding?

You know the answers when we strip away the bullshit.

No one knowingly attracts misery to themselves.

They usually can't see the truth of the matter because they've fed themselves a nice, steady diet of bullshit.

Does this sound familiar?

Well, I didn't ask for it.

But how did you contribute? Are you taking responsibility for what you said and did?

I didn't say that I wanted to be treated like crap.
But what lasting impression are you leaving...that you are worthless?

I didn't want my life to be this stressful.
But you keep making the same choices.

Who's Really in Control Every Day?

You already know the answer.

I'll save you the time in searching yourself.

YOU.

YOU are in control of who you are and who you SAY YOU ARE.

We talked about the steady diet of bullshit.

When you stop feeding yourself the BS, you are all that's left.

You are the truth.

Yep, the buck stops with you now.

Don't be like me.

I let 12 months take 12 years of my life. During that time, I was not living my purpose. Worse, I let other people tell me that it was okay to have a vice.

Hear me out on this one.

Giving yourself permission to have a vice and acknowledging that you have a tendency toward a particular vice or vices are two separate things.

Not acknowledging your addictions gets you tossed in the gutter. Giving yourself permission to indulge in what destroys you makes you lose everything.

Living our best damn life comes fresh off the heels of receiving and giving honesty.

If I am fucking up and spinning my wheels, I want Kelly to tell me what's going on just the way I would tell her. I care about her enough to be vested in what she does for herself. When you reassure someone, "Oh, hey, that's fine. Go ruin your life because you have an addiction," you're an asshole.

That's fucking black and white.

I'm not interested in going through life with blinders on just waiting for wonderful things to be said about me. I want the undiluted truth, so I can use it to one-up myself every day.

That is my mission: always to be better. I hope after you read this book, and unleash your own dark power; it will be yours, too.

Once you hold yourself accountable, you must tell yourself *I will do what's good for me in spite of the pain.*

To be so good, you must commit to seeing what is wrong with you and what needs fixing.

Stay blind, and you won't see a damn thing but what you want to see...what is convenient for you.

You Need Multiple Tools

As a coach, it's important to have tools of all kinds in your pocket to reach people differently. Not everyone will respond to the same thing.

These methods have been effective in breaking through small and damaging mindsets. Try them yourself and see if they help you.

1. **Meditation** – Yes, guided meditation and listening to music and waterfalls counts.

2. **Positive self-talk** - Leave yourself a funny voicemail on your phone. You know like, "Yo, Aaron, don't forget to pick up dog food and also you are one amazing motherfucker!" You can also play a script in your head when you are trying to kick a habit like "No, smoking is not going to control me anymore. Stay strong!"

3. **Setting boundaries** - Repeat after me: "You don't get to talk to me like that."

4. **Write down what you want** - Study it and commit to it. Once you write down your goals, you are the one who can bring them into existence. Make them real so you can annihilate them.

After you try one or all of the above, there will come a day when you accept your new reality. Even better, your new positive habits won't feel like work anymore. Instead, you'll just be living the life you imagined. Your goals will become your lifestyle. When that happens, you can write out new goals you want to reach and work on hitting those, too.

Remember as we close out this chapter, it's not just action or mindset that make the difference in your life.

It's not just passion.

It's not just pain.

It's combining passion and pain that makes you ultra-successful.

It's time to walk into the life you want. Claim it.

Then, keep going.

And as one of my favorite sayings by Mary Engelbreit goes: "Don't look back. You're not going that way."

Chapter 5: Stop Comparing Yourself to Your Competition

***

You don't have any business comparing yourself to other people.

What do you know about them, anyway? As I mentioned earlier, you only are getting shards of what that person is all about. Again, you see the highs and the lows.

This means you are not qualified to even guess at where a person might be in their life. It would be like deciding survey results without taking into account all the variables or the control factor. When you think about it that way, it doesn't make sense, does it?

Would you ever make a decision to buy a new truck without reading the reviews?

In other words...

You need critical data before you can even begin to think about making a decision.

When you are comparing people to you, do you really think you have all the info you need?

What if the situation was switched?

Someone insisted that they knew you, every part of you. That's a load of garbage, right?

How can anyone know anyone else as intimately as they know themselves?

Ding, ding! You're right; they can't.

No one else is an expert on you.

Yes, this situation DOES apply to you. Even if you tend to make different rules for yourself.

See if this sounds familiar:

"I forgive that person for doing the exact same thing I just did, but I don't forgive myself and am going to rake myself over the coals."

If you are going to play the comparison game, every part of the field must be leveled.

The part where you measure your inadequacies with the person you are comparing yourself to.

The part where you refuse to forgive yourself, means you must refuse to forgive them.

The part where you punish yourself for making mistakes despite the fact you are learning, so you must react in the same way toward the person you are comparing yourself to.

What a twisted-up truth you are telling yourself. Or, more accurately…what a pack of lies.

In short, it's like an algebra formula…what you do to one side, you must do to the other.

This is why comparison is not fair, and when we punish ourselves with it, it's more like comparison cafeteria. "I'll compare what they did to win with my shitty results. But I won't take into account my wins or their fumbles to get to the win."

How the fuck is that fair to you?
Why don't you want to be fair to you, anyway?

Stop contrasting what you have accomplished with someone else who has been in their field or at their undertaking longer than you have.

Stop thrashing yourself for not being a mind reader.

Stop refusing to start again because you are afraid to make another mistake.

What in the holy fuck will you lose when you refuse to engage in this game with yourself?

I'll ask you again, as I have done many times throughout this book: "What are you going to lose by changing what you do?"

You can't start where you are in your life, with your income, your mindset, your drive, your business acumen, etc., and expect to find yourself instantly seated at a roundtable of 9-digit sharks murdering every one of their goals in life.

You have to allow yourself the environment to fuck up.

You have to plan for the fucking up, so there will be no fuck up that is so big it will take you under and drown you.

That goes for everything. Every major endeavor you are out there trying your damnedest to slay, you have to allow room for growth.

Get comfortable fucking up. There's a big difference between that and being a fuckup.

When you train your mind to receive well-intentioned mistakes, you build the fortitude to try again.

Don't believe me?

Look up some of your favorite social media stars and watch or listen to their first videos or podcasts. Even they would agree they sucked. But they KNEW they were GOING TO SUCK and they PLANNED for sucking because SUCKING is part of growth.

A super important part actually.

No one shoots out into the world well-versed, able to anticipate the perfect responses and find the most effective solutions.

Aim for being an expert and fuck up. Yes, you have permission to do that. Just remember the difference between fucking up and being a fuck up like we talked about.

Now, I'm not saying that you should look forward to mistakes. Making mistakes hurts. If we make them in public, we are embarrassed and want the floor to open up and swallow us. Is this because of how shitty we think we are because we failed? Or is it because we don't want other people to think we are dumbasses?

You know the answer, and so do I.

But I'm not going to tell you because this book isn't about spoiler alerts.

I want you to do the work to get to the answers you need that will shove you into the prime spot you need to go—your ideal life.

Here's a question and answer it honestly.

When you make a mistake by yourself—when no one is around to see it—do you waste time sitting there ashamed? Your instinct is not to stop and scold yourself. This is learned behavior. We learn to hate ourselves. We learn to discourage ourselves. We learn to regard errors as bad news, as harming our reputation, or as making us look stupid.

Instead of trying to win the world cup of competition, forfeit the game, stop sulking and look for the lesson.

Who cares what other people are doing when it doesn't affect you? Will you meet your goals faster because you can't detach from your dick-measuring game? That game is costing you progress and is self-sabotaging.

Comparing yourself only creates anger and frustration.

The only positive result of fighting in a perpetual pissing contest is that you can learn to positively challenge yourself to try harder. There is literally nothing else that is worth moping over. Let it go. Put space between yourself and whatever you have decided you will never be as good as—whether that's a person or a company. Find something else to obsess over like:

1. The new technology you figured out this week.
2. Your refusal to spend money on stupid shit.
3. Your new deadlift record.
4. That business class you took.
5. The promotion you went after.
6. Hearing another person's viewpoint.
7. Taking risks in your career or business.
8. Making time to work on your relationships.
9. Helping someone without gaining anything yourself.
10. Literally, anything positive that you have accomplished.

I Recommend the FU Session

One weird practice I have for dealing with the urge to compete is I sit down at my computer, and I let myself lose control. Meaning, I cave into any emotion I am feeling at the shitheads who push my buttons. Now, understand, I don't get into fights with people and call them names. I don't attack them on social media, etc., I simply let myself get angry and outraged.

During this hour, I trash talk my industry rivals and the people who have treated me badly (in my head). I visit their Facebook pages and yell internally that I am clobbering them; I am burying them. That I am not worried about them bypassing my success. Because I know what I am doing every step of the way.

I'm confident as I look out at the view in front of me. I'm not staring down at my feet. My head is held high to make sure I can see miles in front of me. The smaller prizes on my journey and in my peripheral vision are intriguing, sure. We all get distracted along the way. But nothing will tear my eyes from my 5, 10, 15, 20, 25, and 30+-year targets. Nothing is that intoxicating that it's worth me giving up what I really want. Especially not engaging in a battle with people who are not worth it.

So, I get it out of my system. I make sure that my eye is on the prize of my choosing. That the allure to get that pleasure from trolling them isn't out of control. The best lesson I have learned from this hour is how to:

Teach yourself to refuse immediate gratification.

Besides, competition obsession is a sign you're playing the short game.

Hanging in there, learning to get up after a loss, returning time and again to your mission has nothing to do with competition.

You are too busy keeping your eyes on your own lane to even care about what is going on next door.

Is your time worth so little that you are willing to give it away for free?

That's what you're doing when you lose focus. You're stealing time from yourself.

Speaking of stealing, that's what a former trainer tried to do to me. He demanded more money and threatened to steal all my clients. When I didn't take the bait, he left to work at a different gym. Four gyms and no one else "seeing his worth" later and he still ain't shit. P.S., two clients left, over 2000 strong by the time this book comes out. I guess that's the difference between focusing on what others do or what you can control—as well as the work you put in.

10/10 would highly recommend the daily FU session.

But why?

So many of us do everything we can to avoid being angry, betrayed, hurt, jealous, etc. I'm talking about the really ugly emotions that everyone does their best to hide from—especially men.

That's why I schedule that time to let that fury bubble up and overflow, to be ticked off, to internally rage. We all need to acknowledge these feelings. When we suppress negative tendencies, that is when we get into trouble.

A feeling that you shove down your throat doesn't disappear.

No, it expands and takes over your body. It taints every cell. The wrath compounds, making it harder to wrestle into submission. Every person has been there, battling back shame that rises to the surface, shame that comes from being a normal reactive person.

This is the shame of being human.

How fucking destructive can we be that we are chiding ourselves for having instinctual feelings?

The key to the success of the fuck-you-exercise is to make sure you put a time limit on your anger—or whatever feeling is trying to strangle you. Let that emotion leave your body when the time is up. You can't stay stuck in a such a vengeful and agitated state. You don't want to carry over the intensity that you escalated from purposely turning up your darkness.

The goal is to practice conditioning your mind to control *what it wants to experience* as you bleed out the steam and pressure during the fuck-you-hour. When you use the fuck-you-hour regularly, it helps you get out of bed. It fires your pistons and launches you out the door.

No more slamming the lid on letting loose, on being allowed to get out your rage. On exercising your right to mentally strong arm your opponent.

Different kinds of mindset strokes for different folks, but you can practice mental fitness while still holding onto what makes you, you. For me, there's no other more effective way to move through what I need to. I just have to get it out. One monstrous immersion into the land of "fuck yous."

It's better than the alternative of me boiling in my outrage and revenge-focused lather. It's better than storming around and making other people uncomfortable. It's better than accidentally fucking up relationships because I couldn't get a handle on my shit.

I didn't like living that way, and I didn't like not being dialed into how I needed to help people.

I thank God for the fuck-you hour and productive internal Hulk smashing.

If you STILL can't get your head out of someone else's ass even using the fuck-you-hour, try this surefire-as-fuck competition hack: close your eyes, picture your rival, and say this to yourself: *I PRAY THAT YOU TRY TO BEAT ME.*

It works.

I figured out what a game-changer this was quick enough when that very same mindset took me from $0 to $3M in 2.5 years.

It's that proven.

At the end of 2018, I was stuck in a rut for a minute. I couldn't get my competition out of my head even though I knew stewing over him was a waste of time. With 12 days left in 2018, I whipped the shit out of that punk. Learning what I was capable of was imprinted in my mind again.

Never again would I rent out my intellectual real estate.

Chapter 6: Getting Right With Your Ego

✲✲✲

Why do we run from the ego?

Over time society has assigned the ego a negative association.

People use it when they are insulting each other: "Okay, egomaniac!"

They use it when they are describing a person they can't stand: "Her ego is really out of control."

We have been groomed to believe that taking pride in ourselves is wrong.

Are you actually comfortable sharing what you have accomplished?

You know this is an exercise that many life coaches recommend, right? The healthy brag?

That's because just as there is power in darkness; there is also power in ego.

A well-functioning ego that is.

First, let's talk about the differences between a healthy ego and an unhealthy ego.

Psychology Today[1] has this to say about it:

Healthy Pride	Unhealthy Pride
"Healthy pride is about self-confidence, reflecting an intrinsically motivating "can do" attitude." When you are in this place, your achievements will be "richly satisfying."	"Those with unhealthy pride, however, may be incentivized to succeed." But… "They're inordinately *driven* to succeed—and repeatedly, because they can't really internalize individual triumphs." In case that's clear as mud, they mean that even if you are nailing your goals, you don't accept your wins as fact. So, you keep trying to do more, not because the sensation of achieving is irresistible, but because you want too badly to win, *even though you already are.* You know these peeps, also. They are likely the ones you avoid because you can't stand their cockiness.
"Healthy pride represents a positive notion of self-worth, and it's based on a history where personal effort and expenditure of energy led to success." Let me break this down: People have learned that repeating specific behaviors leads to rewards. So, they keep doing the same thing, and they keep winning, so then they keep doing the same thing. And, I'm sure you see where this is going… These are the people who you might stand back in awe and watch. They are always seeking the best from themselves…kind of like they are gathering information on their winning stats. After reading this, you can get that "their sense of self-worth merits being seen as 'earned.'"	"Opposite this is unhealthy pride, which depicts an overly favorable evaluation of self, based on giving oneself too much credit for accomplishments that, typically, may be rather modest." These people are set on comparing themselves, and they must build up every little thing they do to feel even a little worthwhile to themselves. You might glimpse this in power couples where one of the partners feels less than, and so they need to constantly pipe up about their own great deeds…which might be more like a household chore…

---

[1] "8 Crucial Differences Between Healthy and Unhealthy Pride." Psychology Today. Accessed June 12, 2019. https://www.psychologytoday.com/us/blog/evolution-the-self/201609/8-crucial-differences-between-healthy-and-unhealthy-pride.

Darkside Dichotomy

Healthy Pride	Unhealthy Pride
"Healthy pride is assessed in an assertive fashion, and it's most often conveyed implicitly." Simply: you do the thing. You shut up about doing it and don't feel the need to holler about your charity from the rooftop.	"...unhealthy pride is far more aggressive—and explicit." It is not a declaration of competence, but of "personal superiority." This egomaniac is better than you. They will dance around you, and no matter what you share about yourself and what you have done, they will make sure you don't leave the conversation feeling like an expert. That title belongs to them. If you want to play a little game, challenge everything they say, and watch their head explode.
Here's a throwback from my last chapter on competition: "...healthy pride has nothing to do with comparing oneself advantageously (and frequently unfairly) to others. "...healthy pride is *authentic*. It's an accurate, realistic estimate of one's abilities."	Unhealthy pride might sound like this: "Look what *I* did!" What they are saying is that "no one *else* could possibly have done such a thing or done it anywhere as well." I mean, it's one thing to be positive and believe that there is a solution for every challenge, but it's another to think you can go from answering the phones at a sales company, for example, to the CEO's position. One word describes this better than any other: grandiosity. People who lean in this direction may be showing traits of narcissism, and they CRAVE hearing that they are better than sliced bread eleventy-billion times a day. This is another reason why people with this tendency fail—they set the bar too damn high, and they will never reach it. This is the adult version of your kid yelling, "Daddy, did you see that dive I did into the pool? Wasn't it great? Watch me on the highest dive now, Daddy. I'm going to be better than anyone ever in the whole wide world!" (Insert maniacal laughter.)

Healthy Pride	Unhealthy Pride
"As understood by experts, healthy pride relates to a person's acting pro-socially." These peeps get out of the house, engage in conversation, meet new friends, forge connections, and "encourage and galvanize others."	"But one endowed with unhealthy pride would imply—or outright proclaim—that what they did could only have been done by them and (they) actively discourage others from following their example." The worst fear these people have is that one day, the whole world will know they are a sham and that other people are better than they are in all ways. See also: classic bully.
"Those with healthy pride motivate and inspire others to take their lead and join them." These are the true leaders you want to align yourself with. The ones who dig collaboration, who push you to find the strengths in yourself that might get overshadowed. These people love to lift you up and get high off seeing you hit your aims. Pro tip: surround yourself with people like this. Be people like this. Bonus if you rock this personality trait: others will be drawn to you since you present no threat to their ego.	Oh, damn. We all know the negative to this positive. This is the sue-happy schmuck who puffs up their chest when they think someone has done them wrong. They are the BTK murderers of the world shouting at the little girl and her tiny dog to get off their lawn.
"Healthy pride isn't egocentric." Of course, it's not. That's the opposite of healthy, which we'll get to in a minute. When you model the behavior of this kind of person, it is not only your triumphs that will make you swell with pride; it's *everyone's*. These people LOVE seeing others overcome and don't believe in luck, but hard work.	You know the other guy. He's the one who doesn't want to see you quit smoking. If you slip up and have a smoke at the end of the day, he's right there with the lighter, chuckling about how "I knew you couldn't do it, bro." His actions might make you feel like he understands where you are coming from and that he accepts you for you...but his shaky, shriveled ego can't stand to see you change and leave him behind.

I know what you're thinking—and I was thinking the same damn thing. *There are a lot of layers to the ego onion!*

I like to compare the ego to the brain because they are both entities that enable a person to access tremendous power.

Like the brain, you can go full tilt insane on surrendering yourself to the dark side. You can open up every black portal and walk right the fuck through. You can challenge yourself to be diabolical (and maybe scare the shit out of yourself in the process!) You can hurt people, use them, slay their spirits and drive, abuse them, and mentally fuck them over.

It's such a fucked-up trip!

But there is always a method to the madness of darkness.

If you're afraid of your darkness, remember you control your actions. This distinguishes you from being a psychopath. If you doubt what I say, let me assure you, I leaned into darkness, and if I hadn't, you might not be reading this book.

On the opposite end of the spectrum is all the light, all the possibility, all the growth, miraculous thoughts, the discoveries and empowerment you can fathom. You can astound yourself with what you learn and walk around in the world with your brain WIDE OPEN to receive information of all sorts. You can order your ego to stand down and get receptive.

Every day can be like winning the mental lottery.

That is how much power we have.

Can you see how the ego would be similar?

It is given to us unmolded and unprogrammed. We begin to feed it the beliefs we gather through our lives based on what we have experienced, how we have been supported (or not), the love we have received (or not) and how much we have allowed ourselves to learn what we are capable of (or not).

Both the brain and the ego govern our actions.

One of my favorite stories about the power of the ego comes from a GM of mine. One day, he told his staff, "If you don't think you're the best, no one else will pay you money to do what you do." His lesson was that you want to avoid thinking, *yeah, I could do it, but there is another guy who is better.* If someone asks you if you're the best, this is your only answer: "Yes, you're fucking right. I AM the best."

I picture the words "pride" and "ego" written side by side with a line drawn between them. That's because in my mind there is a thin line between the two. Modern programming means you can't take pride in what you do, and you should put a leash on your ego.

I disagree. Feed your ego healthy messages like the eight examples discussed above. No one else should be able to give what you give. No one wants second best, and there is not one single motherfucker in this world who gives a shit who won the playoffs. The dark side of my ego wants to challenge you to ask someone if I'm wrong, lol.

Ego Positioning

When I meet a new client, I position myself for a few reasons.

Here's the scenario: a client walks over to me. It's their first day. I introduce myself and then tell them I am the LeBron James of fucking fat loss. I do this because I'm suddenly and immediately unforgettable. By associating myself with such a badass with such an impressive record, I am implying to the client in the first couple of sentences that we share, that I have an impressive record, too. Taking this approach also scores me points because it lightens the mood. The healthy ego doesn't take things as seriously. When you have an ego firing on all cylinders, you want people to feel comfortable around you.

Positioning myself as an expert also allows me to reassure my client. I hope they feel good because seeing them hit weight or fitness goals is an unbelievable boost. It sounds almost selfish, but this is a demonstration of a healthy ego in action.

My ego positioning means:

I am centered in gratitude and service.

I am interested in making sure people feel confident and empowered.

I am all-in on their wins and celebrate HARD with them when they hit it!

And when I commit to myself this way, I win by default.

***

When I moved from West Michigan to South Florida, I knew four people.

The whole premise of moving was that an old client was going to fund me the gym I was opening, and I was going to pay him a set amount of money per year in exchange. He said, "I'll loan you the money to open the gym. You just go down there and get it started. I know you'll be great."

So, I did.

I got a part-time job in Fort Myers, while I was trying to get the gym up and running.

Time went on with me holding down this schedule until we were a week away from closing on the location. At this particular site, one of the other tenants was a cross-fit gym. We don't target the same people, but the owner hadn't asked his permission to occupy the space, and he had a non-compete in his lease. A week before we were supposed to sign, the cross-fit owner pretty much came out and said, "Fuck you, you're not opening in this place."

We had to go to my third possibility down the list of potential spaces to even rent a place that was going to work. By then, I was starting to run out of my severance pay. We needed to get the gym opened yesterday. So, we got the lease expedited, but then my broker called me on the Tuesday of the week we were scheduled to sign the lease. She said, "Hey, Thursday morning we're going to sign the lease. Go ahead and call your financier, so you're good to go."

Well, I called the person providing the financing, and he backed out on me. He literally told me, "Fuck off. I'm not going to invest the money in you." Again, I had moved because he had agreed to help me with the gym! When he dropped this bomb, I was sitting in the parking lot of one of the other gyms in the area, getting ready to work out. I couldn't respond to what he'd said. I just didn't have the words. And I had no idea what to do.

In a panic, I Googled "small business loans," "investors," "startup financing," anything I could think of to try to raise money. It was the first time that I had ever hit this depth of financial fucked-up-ness in my life.

Most people would be like, "This is impossible, there is no way I'm raising 70 thousand dollars in two days. It's not going to happen." I refused to go there in my head. I was not going to quit. A different switch flipped on. *How was I going to come up with the money? How was I going to make it work?*

One of my other clients from Michigan, who had been a client of mine when I was bartending—before I even started working in a partnership to build up the gyms in Michigan popped into my head. She and her husband would come in and dine, and I would take care of them. We developed a really solid relationship. In part because no matter what job I had, I made sure I did my best.

When I opened my first gym with my buddy in Michigan, this client told me, "I'd love to start a workout program." I suggested: "Why don't you try mine?" She ended up becoming a client at the gym for years. Before I left for South Florida, she wanted to take me out for lunch. At the table, after ordering our drinks, she set down her menu and started to talk. I lowered the menu to meet her eyes. "Hey, if you ever need anything, I love you," she said as I smiled in response. "I want to thank you for everything you've done for me," I told her how much she meant to me, too; the server returned with our drinks; we ordered and then finished lunch. In the back of my mind, I knew that she had money since her husband was an inventor in the dental industry.

As I sat in my car in the baking parking lot, my head in a mess over what had happened, I thought of her, and remembered:

She always said if I needed anything... But fuck, 70 thousand dollars is a massive ask... Still, as long as there's a door open, I'm not going to close it.

I called her sobbing on the phone and told her exactly what had happened. That I was fucked; I was going to have to go home with my tail between my legs. At that point, I didn't know what else to do. Before I could even figure anything out, she said, "What's your address? The check's in the mail."

She didn't ask for terms; she simply said, "We'll figure all the rest of this shit out later. Don't reschedule. I'll overnight it right now."

Sure as shit, there was a 70-thousand-dollar check in my mailbox the next day. It took me six months to pay her back, and I didn't take a salary until every penny had been repaid. When it was time to send in the last payment, I flew up to give her the rest of the money because I wanted to hand her that check personally.

After we had exchanged a warm hug, I stepped back, and looked into her eyes with tears in my own and said, "If you want a percentage, if you want a bunch of money back, I don't care, please just tell me. You've changed my life, so thank you."

She waved her hand in the air and smiled. "I never wanted anything back, Aaron," she said. "But there is one thing that you can do for me. If you are put into the position to help someone else, remember this moment and do it for them." She squeezed me in a brief hug again, and when she let me go, said, "I don't want a dollar more than the 70 thousand that you borrowed."

That was one of the most unreal luck stories I've ever lived or heard.

For all the bad shit I had gone through in my life, it's one of the most amazing events that's ever happened to me.

I tell my staff all the time, "You do not know who's going to walk into the gym. It might be an angel in disguise for you. You have no idea who it is; you don't know what they're going to look like. There's going to be a point where you're going to want to accomplish something huge in your life, and they're going to be there to help you if you do a good job. So, do a good job all the time."

That was honestly one of the most humbling, and blessed, moments of my entire life.

I think about it at least once a day, and I am still giving thanks.

At the same time, I realize how different my life would be right now if I had never had the guts to ask for what I needed.

I don't know if I would know that Aaron.

Even today, I ask myself *what would I be doing now if I had believed the opinion of the guy who was supposed to first finance me? What if I had just agreed "Yeah, you're right. I suck. I should just go back to Michigan."*

Do you know how hard it is to ignore the opinion of people around you, especially people who have achieved more than you?

It's psychological murder.

Why No One's Opinion Matters

I tell my team the reason I don't mind how big a target is on my back, or how much attention people give me, is because I share all my faults and weaknesses. I preach about it on Facebook. I don't have one skeleton in my closet. No one can say, "But did you know he's a shady asshole?" I live my life in the open. I've already confessed everything. I've given you all the ammunition you ever need. I am not a perfect human being, far from it, and I proudly own that.

I'm just telling you my story because it's the right thing to do.

We all need to know what each other are learning along the way. Whether I'm right or I'm wrong, you still have to make a decision on what you're going to do.

You can read my whole fucking book and get an insight into all my experiences, but if you don't look in the mirror and make a decision about who you are, and you don't promise to yourself to forget anyone's opinion who doesn't matter, you won't get very far. You won't get out of that parking lot. You'll be stranded with no money and no idea how to tunnel the fuck out. I know that's exactly what you don't want because you are still reading. That means you are looking for more. You are wishing for more every day...you are even searching for the tools in this book to help you get to the place you dream about.

A coach I know is going through a divorce, and I told him, "Dude, you would have done this six months ago, but you were worried about what your parents were going to think. It's affecting your job and every other area of your life. I get that this is a big decision, but at the end of the day, you're the one who has to face yourself and say 'I'm not happy. This isn't the person that as I grow will be the right one for me.'"

It's unbearable even to think that way.

However...

If you don't get clear and confirm to yourself what you really need, you will never have it.

The opinions of the people who you allow in your ear have to get smaller, and smaller, and smaller. The bigger you get, the more you need to tighten up your circle. Get clear on the mindset of who you're letting into your head because it's going to mess with you.

As you grow, strive to care less about people's opinions, and more about your mission. Surround yourself with people who can help you uphold your mission. The more you do this, just like the law of attraction, the more this phenomenon will make itself known in your everyday life.

One of our clients, who had been great to work with up until about two months ago has turned into a complete bitch. She's lost 60 pounds so far. After the weight dropped off, she wanted a rate that she didn't qualify for anymore because she's not a student any longer. Since that happened, she's decided she isn't taking our classes, and she's pissed because we were going to increase her price back to the normal rate.

She was so pissed she wrote a long-ass post on Facebook about how I'm a fucking dickhead. Of course, my wife and staff got all up in arms. But I really don't give a shit what client #1483 thinks about me in the scheme of life.

Let's put this into perspective: I've got over 1500 clients, and they pay me 150 bucks a month. I promise you by the end of next year; I'm not even going to remember she fucking exists.

I push myself when it comes to situations like this, and I urge you to do the same. If I'm not going to remember her next year, why the hell do I give a shit if she likes me or not? We treated her well and helped her reach her fitness goals, but we're not going to be bullied into giving her a discount she doesn't qualify for. That wouldn't be fair to the other members.

Stand your ground. People who cycle out of your life do so for a reason.

Every day, I have two choices. I can wake up tomorrow; I can keep working, and keep trying to help more people. I can keep writing this fucking book, or I can say, "A client talked shit about me today, and I have to quit." It sounds so immature when we say it out loud, doesn't it? But so many people let someone else's crappy (and inaccurate) opinion freeze them in place and prevent them from going any further. We default to this thought: *oh, I can't do this, because what if this person thinks I'm an idiot?*

People are going to think you're fucking stupid. That's part of life. You can't control it anyway, so why worry about it? I'm going to think you're stupid if you don't follow your fucking path. Whenever you do that, and you allow something else to sway you from the path, I will *always* shake my head and think: *you're not following what you are meant to be doing.* Yeah, this is hard, but if you let your fears win I will think you're a fucking cop-out, Yes, you might have other people who look at you and give you an out. They might say some bullshit like *stop trying to shine too bright or do too much.* Where is the value in that? You want the people on the other side of the coin who say, "Dude, you should be doing this. You *should* be staying on track. *Because you want to stay on track.*"

You want the people around who will never validate what your exhausted ass sometimes hopes to hear: *It's okay to quit. No one will know. Just step back quietly and disappear.*

Does that message seem congruent with blasting through your goals?

That's the dumbest question in the world. I hope to God you have the right answer for it. Look at all the people who achieve mighty feats. The weightlifters, the world record holders. They are steel when they walk out there to fucking own their focus and effort. There is not one champion ALIVE or DEAD who has ever had a pep talk like: *Take a break, sport. The ball will be there tomorrow. Oh, you feel sick? Better take a breather.*

Fuck that.
Fuck that.
Fuck that.

No winner is EVER made that way. So, if you are on a winning path, embrace the fucking pain and wallow in it.

As you upgrade, you should be upgrading the people you're around.

The people who are ahead of you will never look at you and say, "You're a dipshit to try; you should quit." It's always the people who are behind you who try and discourage you because they want you to join the pity party. They love that fucking pity party. Oh, you get great attention at the pity party...it's just the wrong kind that disproves the truth you are trying to find out about yourself, the power you are trying to set loose in your life.

The further ahead of people you get, the more people that you pass, the more you're going to hear that you should stop and join the rest of the stragglers in life. When you're passing more and more people, they all have a fucking opinion.

This is all you have to do when this happens:

Not care.
Not listen.
Not take it in.

Be the guy with his eyes on mowing the lawn while the house behind him blows up. Have that be your goal to focus so intensely like a laser drilling through wood, that you NEVER stop your course!

Your job is to be better for you. Period. Keep your eyes on your lane, on your bobber, on the road, or whatever analogy you want to tell yourself.

It's an amazing feeling to know <u>you're fucking perfect just as you are</u>.

It takes some people 70 years to learn this about themselves; it takes other people seven years. Once you find that feeling, protect it. Don't wonder *is this truly it?* You fucking know it is. Just set your mental man-eater dog in front of that feeling and defend its right to exist at all costs.

As we close this chapter, I know if you've been paying attention that you now know the ego possesses power. But if you don't know how to put it to work for you, you'll end up offending everyone you meet by being a stuck-up ass, or you'll hide in a corner waiting for life to end. When you respect the power of your ego and use it as you are supposed to: to hold up the highest version of you, then you will see your purpose.

But know this: if you don't have a purpose, nothing else will matter.

Finally, keep your ego in check by putting yourself in situations where you're not the smartest person. When you do this, it gives your ego a hearty, meaty meal to feast on: humility, coexistence, and respect. It's how you keep growing the way you are supposed to. To give back to yourself and others.

Chapter 7: Giving Back Leads to Abundance

***

So many people set out on the abundance path, believing that when they find the key to abundance and living the life they have always dreamed of, riches will come flooding into their house. They won't have to work another day in their life. They can pick out any house on the block, go up to the homeowner and say, "Everything has its price. How much to get you to sell?"

These same people are very disappointed to find out that reaching your goals (and staying there) is nothing like that. Luck runs out. And even when you scale your business and systematize it, you can still lose everything—if you don't know how to hang onto it.

Unless you release scarcity and self-limiting beliefs, you will stay exactly where you are.

This is no BS either.

It's actually scientific. Think about energy. You know that you can never extinguish energy. If the vessel holding it dies, the energy moves on. It has to go somewhere. If you are wondering if I pulled that theory out of my ass, I didn't. This discovery and quote belong to Einstein: "Energy cannot be created or destroyed, it can only be changed from one form to another."

I know what you're thinking! *WTF is Aaron going off on now?*

Stay with me.

Abundance is the same way. Abundance is at its base, energy. But in the case of attracting abundance, we have to be reciprocal. If you are trying to attract it, the surest way to draw it to you is by giving something away. When you live with a charitable and loving intention, the abundance finds you. But before I go on and prove my point, let's go back in time to a Christmas when I was a little boy.

***

December 2003

I was 17 years old, and we were living in total desperation; my mom was unable to figure out how we would have Christmas. My brother, Pete, and I understood that there would be no presents and even though that made us quite sad, we were living the proof of why there wouldn't be. When paying rent is a struggle, you kind of figure out the rest. I was so alienated from other kids in this way. Mom tried her best to provide for us, but even after selling almost ALL her possessions, it was going to be a stretch. We all knew it but didn't talk about it much.

Mom motioned for us to come close one winter night as snowflakes hit the window and melted in a trickling river down the pane.

Pete and I inched nearer to her, and she grabbed our hands and covered them with hers. Her touch was cold and dry. I felt the strangest urge to protect her even as she told us the bad news about Christmas.

"I just can't do it," she whispered as her voice caught on the sobs, I knew she was holding back.

"That's okay, Mom," I said around the lump in my throat as I worked to make her tears go away with my acceptance of the truth.

"We already know," Pete said, trying to keep the frown off his face. The faint light in his eyes highlighted zero hope.

My stomach lurched as my mom released our hands and said, "My boys. I promise next year will be better."

I laid in the dark that night and replayed the news in my head. Then I surrendered to it and closed my eyes.

What else could I do?

Let me reassure you the darkness is nothing to fear. When you have hung out in it long enough, your eyes adjust, and you can see all the monsters right down to the hair on their toes.

Then the old saying, "It is always darkest before the light" came true for us.

One particularly hard night, someone knocked on our door. Mom opened it and a woman we had all seen around the neighborhood but didn't know that well handed Mom an envelope crammed with money. Mom's eyes watered as she reached out to hug this woman, but she also knew the right thing to do was to take the money because she had kids who were depending on it. I can imagine, in her eyes, she must have felt like she had let us down. But I can't imagine what it took for her to swallow her pride for her boys. However, I am so grateful she did.

Mom bought us each a small gift and used the rest of the money to catch up on bills and make us our favorite Christmas morning meal: monkey bread.

Now I use Christmas as a motivator.

Even years later, I can still put myself back in that moment and feel Mom's hand in mind and observe the dying light in Pete's eyes.

That's why the Kids' Christmas Campaign was born.

Giving Feeds Success: the Kids' Christmas Campaign

In the last three years, Platinum Fitness has helped 150 kids with a donation of nearly $50K. I don't ever want a child to have to see what hopelessness looks and feels like because their parents are fighting hardships. Kids have it hard enough these days, competing with other children at school over the holidays, dealing with bullying, all the stress of school and don't get me started on peer pressure. The last damn thing they need around the holidays is to feel worse about themselves. Kids who still believe in Santa, when their parents come up short, think that Santa is rejecting them. That's deep pain for a kid, and it breaks my heart.

The Kids' Christmas Campaign children receive WHATEVER THEY ACTUALLY WANT: Xboxes, bikes, the shoes, and clothes they dream about. We work off the lists those kids write to make sure they get exactly what they want.

Once the kids are taken care of, we give the parents gift cards they can use for food. One of the sad facts I learned when I got involved in giving back to this community is that if kids don't eat at school, they don't eat. We wanted those kids going home and having enough food to fill their bellies.

I recall vividly what it meant to Mom to receive that money to help us. She could buy presents and groceries ahead of time to ease her worries.

Now, I have that same opportunity and from that Christmas Day, giving back just like this and making a difference in kids' lives is all I ever wanted. It feels so good like I am the one who is benefitting the most from giving...and sometimes I wonder if I am!

This past year, I flew home to Michigan and took my mom and brother to dinner where I gave them a wad of money and told them there would be more of the same if they would do something to grow it. I would match it no matter what they decided to do with it to make it work for them.

But there were conditions.

I told them: "If you invest your money, you could have $5000 in your bank account." I had a big-ass smile on my face and tapped the table with my hand to rouse up a little excitement. "Wouldn't that be cool?" I asked Mom as Pete shot me doubtful looks. "The catch is this," I told them: "If you don't make your money grow, don't come ask me for money next year."

I made that rule to teach them that if you have a money problem, it's *your* money problem. Me giving them a grand or two grand, to pay backed-up bills isn't going to fix the issue. The real issue is not knowing how to budget, and how to add value to money or save it.

I laid down this boundary:

If you're okay with not working overtime, not having a second job, and not giving up side activities that cost money and that you love, it doesn't mean I should have to support you.

People take so much pride in, "Well, I have a roof over my head; I have food on the table, and my bills are paid." When I hear that I think *shit...that's all you want? Why don't you want more for yourself? Why don't you want as much for yourself and your family as possible?*

Yes, it's acceptable to live like that, but if you knew there was more out there for you, don't tell me you wouldn't take it. I know you would because we all would if given the shot.

But...you have the shot already. You just have to keep your head down, stay on task, and get there.

Let me also assure you it's okay to want more than you have.

There's nothing weird about wanting to stretch your personal limits and the boundaries of your income. Yes, it's super important to be grateful, to realize how blessed you are to live in America, to have a roof over your head, a car, and a job. I totally agree that you need to be grateful for those things, *but if that's all you want,* you're missing the point of being alive. Every day we get a new chance to prove to ourselves what an incredible badass we are.

If you're still not convinced, this question should get you there. Ask yourself: *is this how I really want to be remembered? Or, is there something more out there for me?*

Don't forget as we wind up this chapter that *giving feeds success.*

You will not see success expanding in the life of the selfish asshole who has an ego and is in it for money. So, take the time to go out and do things for other people. Help them. Work paying forward into your day just like you schedule calls or complete your morning fitness routine.

Some people (and you know who these self-limiting peeps are) feel like they don't want to be on the positive receiving end because then they will be obligated to give back in some way.

First, abundance doesn't work like that. Opportunities don't work like that. You are under absolutely no contract to give back, so if that is one of the reasons you're hesitant to receive, you're playing small, and you no longer have an excuse.

But be ready to stay in the same spot or lose traction if you are walking around with your hands in your pockets—so no money slips out—not to mention your head up your greedy ass.

You *want to give what you can away. You want to help people for the good it does for you (and of course, others). And if you want an endless spout of blessings directed your way—YOU NEED TO GIVE.*

It's a reciprocal effect as you will learn if you decide to be Scrooge McDuck. The universe knows you are taken care of financially when you hoard money, so it won't make it rain all over you because the vibe you're kicking off is that you don't need the money...you don't have a plan for it.

You have enough energy, and so new energy doesn't need to flow in to fill the gap.

As Adam Grant says in his book *Give and Take*, expecting that you need to match, is exactly what it sounds like: it is a matcher mentality.

According to Grant, givers always end up more successful because they give freely without that feeling of *I owe you*. They just do it because that's what they want to do. They don't have expectations. The taker, however, takes without expectations and tries to con people. And the matcher might think *If I give you something you owe me one; you have to give me something in return*. The only people who ever succeed at a massive level are the givers.

Don't cop out and try and convince yourself you are a status-quo person either. You are reading this book because you want to succeed at an elite level.

You know what the fuck you need to do.

Quit making excuses and do it.

Chapter 8: The One Surefire Way to Get Un-Stuck

***

When you're stuck…and we all get stuck…it's a PITA (Pain In The Ass) to get unstuck.

Why? This analogy has always helped me…

Remember when you would ride bikes on the trails or offroad (If you are under 27 probably not, but we used to play outside before Fortnite). If you saw that big rut and went into it, it was almost impossible to get out of. You would have to rip your tire hard left or right to get it over the hump the first time. Getting stuck in any habit, mindset, or ritual is the exact same concept—the first couple of times you have to consciously rip yourself out.

What is cool is, after a dozen times, you can start to see the way out. The edges become skewed. You can pull yourself out of the rut at multiple points. It just takes practice and awareness.

Maybe you've tried what every guru has advised:

1. Focus on your small wins.
2. Do what you know you can do confidently.
3. Change your self-talk.
4. Change your routine.
5. Change the people you hang out with.
6. Meditate.
7. Get a new coach or mentor.
8. (Insert your go-to when-I-get-stuck-I-do-this-response here.)

Once again, this list is missing the surefire action that I take every time I find myself in a place where I can't advance.

Looking for Gratitude

You notice I didn't say, *"Finding* gratitude"? That's because our brains don't know the difference between finding gratitude and merely searching for it.

It's true, and I couldn't fucking believe it when I read it either!

The article, "A Neuroscience Researcher Reveals 4 Rituals That Will Make You Happier," from *Business Insider*[2], points out: "You know what the antidepressant Wellbutrin does? Boosts the neurotransmitter dopamine. So does gratitude."

This proves my point that we have everything we need for our bodies' healing within us already.

Now, before we dive into this holistic stuff, let me also say that it takes an incredibly strong individual to try and try and try and then have enough self-awareness to realize a pattern and seek professional help so they can break it.

Trust me. As someone who learned this lesson the hardest way possible, it can cost you more than you know if you ignore any of the problems you have. They must never be ignored. The whole "double down" on your strength and "IGNORE your weakness" shit is garbage. Your weaknesses make you mortal. Imagine if you had no Achilles heel or Samson hair. So, now that we are heading into some amazing stuff, the warning is this: DO NOT LET THIS SECTION BE A SCAPEGOAT TO ALLOW YOUR WEAKNESS TO OVERCOME YOU.

---

[2] Barker, Eric. "A Neuroscience Researcher Reveals 4 Rituals That Will Make You Happier." *Business Insider*, Business Insider, 30 Dec. 2018, www.businessinsider.com/a-neuroscience-researcher-reveals-4-rituals-that-will-make-you-a-happier-person-2015-9.

To revisit the article: "The benefits of gratitude start with the dopamine system because feeling grateful activates the brain stem region that produces dopamine. Additionally, gratitude toward others increases activity in social dopamine circuits, which makes social interactions more enjoyable."

We have become so quick to grab whatever pill we can to treat our mental funks. What would happen if we engaged in doing specific exercises with our brains to access instinctual healing power instead? You know from reading the beginning of this chapter that what you need to heal is you…and determination.

Remember this point from the article again:

"Know what Prozac does? Boosts the neurotransmitter serotonin. So does gratitude."

Now, add this point:

"One powerful effect of gratitude is that it can boost serotonin. Trying to think of things you are grateful for forces you to focus on the positive aspects of your life. This simple act increases serotonin production in the anterior cingulate cortex."

I translate this to mean that there is no such thing as *seeking gratitude.* There is only *finding it* since you experience thankfulness merely by looking for it.

Try being grateful and (insert any negative emotion here) at the same time. You can't. That means you can't be grateful and stuck at the same time. Cool, huh?

Another article I read talked about how people pick up on the energy of each other. Essentially, we are walking sponges soaking up vibrations…good and bad.

Have you ever noticed that you might be in a good mood, and then when you walk into a room where there is tension, your Spidey Sense immediately picks it up?

Or, how about when you walk into a place that is frenetic with activity? There's a shit-ton of chaos, and instantly you can feel your shoulders rising to hit your ears? Maybe there's too much peopling going on, and you wish everyone would STFU? (My problem is my mouth usually yells that before my brain goes NO.)

You are an electric entity, alive with a roadmap of nerves and little-understood sensory traits.

The point is, when we concentrate on the good in our lives, we REWIRE our brains *and* our energy. And when we do that, we affect everyone in our radius. I take this to mean that we actually have a *responsibility* to watch our emotions, energy and gratitude because there is no such thing as "living in a bubble." Try as we might to establish "personal space," it might be a lie.

If we want to scratch deeper than the surface, here's a scary and thrilling thought, *maybe we are not supposed to be separated from each other? Maybe we aren't supposed to be so guarded? Maybe we are supposed to be in each other's force fields?*

It's certainly food for thought.

When you become grateful, you become part of the ripple. You stay in the now. You appreciate the present and even lessen your anxiety. Why wouldn't you when you are bouncing along happy as a frickin' clam with what you have at that very moment?

What's that old saying that explains mindset in a nutshell?

Something like: "Anxiety is focusing on the future, depression on the past, and peace, the present."

If you are stuck, search for gratitude. You will move beyond your problems into what is going right.

That mere shift in your perspective allows for space to occur and intensity to lessen between yourself and your issues. You need that perspective and distance. Fixate on what you *are dying for,* and it will feel like you will wait forever.

Of course, the hardest part is letting go.

Think back on a time when you were stuck and how you found a resolution. Was it because you nearly had a fucking meltdown obsessing over whatever it was that you thought you needed in that moment? What probably happened is that you were able to walk away and see a different solution out of your problems. In the same way, that abundance *will never come to pessimists; solutions will not reveal themselves when you are not feeling gratitude.* You can't see. You are blind. You can't move one inch ahead *because you won't let yourself.*

Holding onto that hurdle is obviously giving you some kind of reward. But what is it? Are you scared to take action? Are you receiving self-pity? Are you getting attention?

Aren't those ugly fucking questions!?!

But if you drop your defenses and listen to my message; you will see I just might be right.

We run from those dark needs in ourselves. All of us are guilty of this, even me. We train ourselves to do that, as well as everyone around us urges us to ignore our inner needs that don't make us feel prideful.

Get comfy with these nasty feelings and once again, let yourself be a human, would you?

Acknowledge the feeling: *okay, I am stuck, and there is a part of me that needs attention and reassurance right now. That's okay. I wonder if there is a better way to get it?*

THIS is when you start to move mountains in your mind.

This is when you live in peace with ALL OF YOU, and you help yourself get to better places in your head.

You might be reading this and thinking *great, that works for you, Aaron, but I am really stuck. I'm not sure about this.*

If this is how you are thinking, we know one truth for sure: *if you don't challenge yourself to get out of your mental mind trap, you are going to stay there.* I know this with incredible and proven certainty.

Desperation is never the right state of mind to be in when you are searching for solutions. That's why I want you to look for the reasons to be grateful in your life. Gratitude moves you out of that desperate mindset.

And NEVER make a long-term decision based on short-term emotions.

That's one of my favorite sayings. I use it to remind myself to *chill the fuck out and not DO ANYTHING until I have a handle on myself.*

Desperate decisions will likely result in regret. You might make a rash choice to get out of a jam, but you probably didn't think of all the implications involved. Which means, now you have more problems.

If you feel desperate, you have not found the gratitude you need to move out of your harmful (stuck) mindest.

When we are stuck, we get so focused on *getting out of where we are* that we spend far less time figuring out *the right way to get unstuck*.

We confuse our goals.

Desperation also equals fear.

And you damn well know better that you need to do everything possible to avoid making significant decisions in the scarcity mindset.

You will never get ahead this way.

You will reinforce negative and destructive behaviors.

You will re-condition yourself to continue making choices in this state.

You will have no long-term building options.

In other words, nothing sustainable is constructed from the basis of fear and desperation…unless you have crazy luck. And I would argue that that is a slimmer than slim percentage because (and you've heard this) luck comes as a result of preparation and opportunity.

How in the fuck does being stuck result in luck? Say that 10 times fast.

Truth: it doesn't.

To come full circle. When you are stuck, stop what you are doing. Pause your emotions. Throw anger into a chair in the corner. Get it a drink, and get to thinking about what is *right* in your life. Oh, you're frustrated, too? Tell that mofo, frustration to join anger, and they can do shots or something. Here comes fear. You know, that guy is so annoying. Send fear over to hang with the other two losers. You have work to do. Pity wants to join the party. Pity makes my skin crawl. Kick its ass into the corner, too!

Once you're in a better and healthier state of mind, you can join the gratitude ripple. You can get excited again about what you can do—because you are doing it and acknowledging it—versus being stuck.

When you are in the thick of the gratitude ripple, you can pass on the energy that changes the world. You can even be the catalyst to help someone stop *their* dark spiral. Because the more we hold each other up, the more we are held up. Consider it this way: take care of other people so they will take care of you.

Let's see if you can relate to any of these scarcity patterns and limiting self-beliefs that keep you stuck:

1. You are afraid to invest: in business, yourself, your family, relationships, education, parenting, etc. because you can't stop thinking about how you don't have enough time and money and whatever other resources apply to you.

2. You are only capable of doing so much in every area of your life. Major success and goal pulverizing are meant for other people.

3. You are condemned to live a certain life because you don't deserve any better.

4. You will never be able to change your bad habits because you don't have enough will power. But just wait...this list gets darker and more self-shameful (even though it shouldn't)... as shared in the *Power of Positivity:*[3]

5. You don't know how to be happy for other people's success.

6. You compare yourself *all the time* to everyone else.

7. You're worried there isn't enough work to go around. You think that if other people gain something: money, a new job, freelance gigs, etc., that means there is less for you.

8. Subconsciously, you *dig it* when others fail.

9. When you win, you feel like you have beat everyone.

10. When asked why you haven't reached your goals, you come up with negative reasons.

11. It's hard for you to share.

12. You want to be in charge.

13. You can only think of success as a competition and that you must beat out someone to win.

14. You don't focus on long-term goals but just live in the now (this is the making-choices-from-a-desperate-mindset thing we talked about!).

---

[3] PowerofPositivity. "10 Signs Of A Scarcity Mindset ." Power of Positivity: Positive Thinking & Attitude. April 23, 2016. Accessed June 19, 2019. https://www.powerofpositivity.com/10-signs-of-a-scarcity-mindset/.

We jumped deep in the shit, didn't we? Did you notice how easy it is to stay there and not even want to move? How easy it is to let these thoughts convince you that being unable to move is easier?

Nothing is at stake when you are stuck, and although you may hate it, it's easier than the alternative of getting to work to improve your life or tossing your ass out of your pity party.

I'm glad you went there with me.

Two things before we close out this chapter:

1. I want you to remember that of everything we talked about; there is nothing wrong with you feeling any damn way at all. It's so much better to nod at your emotions as they walk by than to run away from them yelling your fool head off. Resist getting stuck because that *hurts* you.

2. When you figure out how you are feeling, then you can figure out how to stop acting like a dumbass in certain circumstances. P.S. I am not talking down to you, I am telling myself this, too...

I have been through this whole mental circus and still struggle every damn day.

You don't want to be afraid to move forward.

You don't want to be suffocated by self-doubt.

You don't want to keep insulting yourself because you get a reward from self-pity.

You don't want to worry you will never win and that you can't figure out success.

You don't want to feel like a wuss because you dare to be a human, FFS.

You don't want to not grow and or amaze yourself.

However, you are stuck; I know you HATE it.

So, take the steps to move!

Seek gratitude.

Gain perspective.

Shut down the pity party.

Get honest about your thought patterns and kick that scarcity mentality in the ass! Then get off your ass and do something, anything to break the pattern. You don't even have to be good at what you want to do. The simple act of breaking the pattern of doing the same thing is enough to move you forward.

Don't Pay Abuse Forward.

There are enough broken people walking around on this planet fucking with other people's energies, moods, and goals. Don't be one of them!

Don't break another person because, in your head, you are so weak that bullying is the only way to feel better about yourself.

Trust me, I see it in my own life. The more you move into your power, the more attention will be put on you by the bottom feeders in your life. They will always have their opinions and will blast you every chance they get.

Here is the secret though: you can outwork them.

Keep putting together action after action, good deed after good deed, and step after step. This is the reason everyone hates the Patriots in football except Patriot Nation. They win. They execute a game plan. They don't feed the trolls. They just work toward an outcome until it is reached. Do they always win? No, and when they lose, the bottom feeders pile on, but Tom Brady described it best. "The reason they are fans is that they are in the stands, they aren't on the field playing the game."

Whether it's fair or not, this fact is true: fans will always remain in the stands because they are too scared to play in the field.

They are scared, just like you.

The only difference is you stepped onto the field. So, play the game; and if you are going to play the game, WIN.

Dominate.

Run that mother fucking score up.

Don't justify your fears.

Don't grow complacent with your life because before you know it, it will be over.

You'll be staring down the barrel of an agonizing hospice stay or some other damn tragic circumstance, and it will be too late.

You picked up this book, so don't lie about what you want.

Stuck is a state of mind.

Get the fuck out of it.

Chapter 9: Accepting Help is a Superpower

✳✳✳

If you have found my book hard to read because it got a little too real for you, I think you will like this chapter.

As the title suggests, accepting help is something that not a lot of people have the ability to do. I think of it as a superpower.

I'm not gonna lie either. I had a bitch of a time asking for help when I was younger. I thought I was supposed to do everything myself and then puff up my chest like "No one helped me at all!"

What is the point of that? Why do we get so stuck on doing everything ourselves, and feel such misplaced pride? Society feels pride in it, too. You'll read headlines that use words like "Self-Made Man," "Self-Made Billionaire." Look at Kylie Jenner who made the cover of a business mag because she was the youngest "Self-Made Billionaire."

First of all, excuse me? She is not a "self-made" anything. She has a whole team behind her. Her story chafed a whole bunch of asses because credit was not being given where it's due. Her momager, Kris Jenner is a branding genius who pushed her child into BILLIONAIRE STATUS! She has made her entire family into superstars.

Teamwork Makes the Dream Work

It takes a team of people to accomplish great things. Yes, of course, individuals can reach incredible feats on their own, but for the most part...it does take an ensemble.

A salesperson's close isn't solely his win. His sales manager has provided the support, training, and encouragement he needed. The business where the salesperson works provides access to products and/or services as well as a physical location to work.

When I am advising clients on their new healthier paths, one-million percent of these people find more success when they have the support of others.

It's easier for a person kicking any habit to do it with their circle cheering them on.

When people show up at the gym determined to get toned or lose weight, their trainers can cheer them to the finish line.

We have this displaced idea of when we should use a team and when we should fly solo.

In some instances, people want to own their accomplishments. In other cases, it's implied that we need a team and shouldn't go it alone.

I'm arguing that we are never solely alone in striving to meet our goals.

Your wife is there.

Your kids.

Buddies.

Family.

Neighbors.

Whoever you have on your team...they are there thinking of you and coaxing you to keep going.

If they aren't rooting you forward, then they are waiting for you when you get home to hear all about it.

It is nearly impossible to exist in a bubble in life.

People are always around us. Even when we think they aren't. Even when we think our presence doesn't impact anyone else.

You make impressions when you are not even trying to. You are leaving people with memories of who you are and denting the world with the imprint of you.

Because you are not forgettable, you will always have help, and you will always be able to ask for help.

Unless you are in extreme isolation.

Because most of the world is behind in accessing the superpower of asking for help, when you practice asking for what you need, you come out ahead.

Giving vs. Asking for Help

Let's talk about why giving help and asking for help feel so disconnected before we go any further.

Giving help or even contributing to a charity of some sort feels good, and what feels good serves us.

While we have committed a wonderful act of generosity, at the base of this gesture is what feeds us.

We feel good when we give.

We like the feeling of helping others when they are in a jam.
It makes us feel productive, or as if we have contributed meaningfully.

The point is...it makes us feel so good...it is nearly selfish.

To sum up this confusing backward statement:

Giving is almost selfish, and so is asking for help?

How is that even possible?

Our minds have such a tremendous capacity to reason and compare it will make your head spin.

Stay with me anyway.

Asking for help is regarded as being selfish, weak, a leech, lazy, and a whole other list of insults that I don't have enough paper to write out.

Asking for help also means that we have to get vulnerable with ourselves and other people.

Immediately, we need to admit that we can't do something by ourselves. When we have this come-to-Jesus talk with ourselves, it doesn't feel good. It feels like we have failed. We haven't taken care of ourselves. We haven't planned well. We aren't smart enough or resourceful enough. In fact, our internal conversations all come down to the fact that we can't do whatever it is we are seeking to do alone.

Why in the world is it a bad turn of events to discover information about ourselves? That's all it is. We now have new information about ourselves, and we can use it to become better, to work more easily and readily with others, and to solve our problems.

This discovery is not a bad thing.

After you realize you need help, then you must be humbled enough but confident enough to ask for it.

This requires that you trust the person or people you are asking for assistance. Trust is a big deal, and it is the root of why so many people refuse to ask for help and why they stubbornly lock up their communication and deny themselves what they need most.

When I receive help from anyone—which I do multiple times a day—I think about the effect it has on the person or people doing the providing. I know they feel good because I feel great when I help other people.

Accepting Help Requires Vulnerability and Trust

It is a privilege and an honor to see a person's vulnerability.

The safe space that they provide for you has just as much meaning to them as it does for you. In their eyes, they are seen as loyal, valuable, trustworthy, and as a special member of your tribe because you trusted them.

That's a big deal.

If you own and operate your own company, for instance, have you figured out yet that you are limited by the physical, emotional, and mental constraints you have to balance alone? You can only close so many deals before you need someone else to step in. You can only work so many hours and expend so much mental energy and concentration. At some point in the process of scaling, it is inevitable that to do more, you must recruit people to help you. You must delegate and own tasks together.

Don't underestimate the value of collaboration either. That's why the saying "Two heads are better than one" is true. You bring to the table only what you know, what you imagine, and envision, your experiences, your attitude, etc. When another person enters the picture, they bring their own signature list of these things to add to yours to give you both greater perspective and strength.

The significance of two or more people working together can't be minimized.

More brains, more ideas, more determination, and a compounded belief in the project and each other. There's no way that state of affairs could be achieved by one person alone.

As John Maxwell said: "One is too small a number to achieve anything great." Remember, you will never get to any real level of success if you don't ask.

How to Ask for Help

I almost laughed out loud, typing that subheading when I wrote it. What a simple concept and the fact that we even have to discuss it is ridiculous.

But I have found in my coaching, mentorship, and training when I provide specific examples that people can use in the areas where they struggle, they really appreciate it.

Besides, who's going to raise their hand and say: "I need to know how to ask for help"?

I'll answer that for you: no one ever.

So here goes…10 Ways to Ask for Help

1. "Hey, can you give me a hand?"
2. "Can I borrow your (brain, arms, back) for a sec?"

3. "How did you do that?"
4. "So, I'm stuck."
5. "What do you think of this? Because I feel (this way)."
6. "Can you figure this out?"
7. "This must be the new math."
8. "Would love your opinion here…"
9. "Did I miss anything?"
10. "What would you add?"

We get stuck on the idea that we have to make ourselves a lowly creature crawling on its belly if we want help. That we have to diminish ourselves or admit we are a dope. But none of that is true.

Asking for help can be conversational and super low pressure.

Besides, we are all allowed to catch a break. And to get that break we need each other. This is a definite circumstance where you can't go it alone.

Going after help also means that you will not sit around and wait anymore, stuck in your pride about not speaking up.

You might also not seek help because you think if you do all of sudden you have turned on the reciprocal train. Maybe you think: *I don't have time to return the favor.* Maybe you are even secretly annoyed at the idea that someone would help you because while you need it now, you have no idea when you will be able to pay back the person.

That's assuming they are looking for a payback, but generous people who give for the right reasons usually aren't.

Just as we talked about the givers, takers, and matchers earlier in the book, givers always end up more successful because they give without expectation. The taker takes without thinking of the person giving, and if you wanted to identify a con man, he would be a taker. Matchers need the relationship to be reciprocal.

When you surround yourself with the right people—the givers—they will pitch in without trying to make you feel bad about needing them.

I needed help writing this book, and there wasn't ever a minute where I regretted reaching out. It was a goal that was important to me, and I knew I needed to be open to learning what I had to do to get it done.

But what if I hadn't done that?

Would you be reading it?

What if I hadn't accepted the help for the gym when I wasn't feeling the strongest and was in tears in my car?

It would have been easy to ignore what I needed to do, what was hard—reaching out—to convince yet another person to believe in my dream as much as I did.

Why are you resisting reaching out?

.

Chapter 10: Being True to Yourself

Aaron Nash

***

Let's get right to the gritty core of this message. Being true to yourself means being 100% true to the man or woman in the mirror. It means you don't give a fuck what anyone else thinks about you.

I work hard to make myself an open book because I don't want someone to go digging in my personal life and find a scrap of truth they can use against me. I beat them to the punch. I hang out all my filthy laundry, so there are no questions about what kind of person I am.

I will make myself the largest target possible, so people have no doubts about my integrity.

Over the course of my life, I have learned that if you don't forget other people's opinions of you, you won't be able to go very far. You will always be trying to live up to someone else's expectations of you.

Is the way your mom thinks of you the way you think about yourself?

Of course, not.

Besides, if you guys had the same opinion and wanted the same goals for you, that would be pretty codependent. It's not healthy for you to base your decisions on what another person wants for you. Or to seek their approval.

But why is it so hard to let go of the unhealthy place we go to find validation or approval?

Because you can't find what you need in yourself.

If you could, you would have moved forward by now. Maybe you would be in a different place. Maybe you would have taken a step toward the destination where you want to go.

We lose so much time when we are frozen in place and awaiting the go-ahead from other people *who have nothing to do with us. Who aren't us.*

Before you know it, six months can pass you by, and you are no further ahead than where you have been *for years.*

I remember this rule of thumb about being true to myself if I start to put too much weight into other people's opinions of me:

"The more people's opinions you allow in your ear, the more you have to get smaller and smaller." ~Me

In simpler terms, if you don't actively work on minimizing other's voices, they are going to mess with you and your life trajectory.

One of the nicer benefits I have found about expanding and deepening your mindset is, the more you grow, the less you will care about other people, but the more you will care about your mission.

When you are in this mental space, you will stand in your truth facing the right direction every single day. Moving in the right direction over and over again forms a habit and will prepare you for your most meaningful success.

I am talking about the kind of success where you sit back and say, "My life will never be the same." The kind of success where you can't unlearn the pivotal points that led you to a new reality. You know too much, and you can never return to the place you couldn't wait to get out of.

Have you ever experienced that feeling? Where you just know you have hit a milestone in your life that will forever push you forward to bigger and better?

It is this kind of mindset, day in and day out that guides successful people. It is more painful for these types of people to take the easy way out.

In fact...

It is torture.

At this point in their development, this motivated person can't abandon ship. Too much is riding on what they will or won't do. Successful people answer to themselves and don't care what anyone else thinks of their clean or dirty laundry.

What's the Deal with Overcomplication?

When you say out loud: "I can wake up tomorrow, or I can quit," It sounds so stupid and simple. When you break the sentence down in this way, the choice seems obvious. Why would you quit? Unless a catastrophic event happens, you know quitting is not the way forward. Quitting is not the route you want to take.

Who cares if another person thinks you can't do what you are setting out to do?

That's a limiting way to think, and their opinion doesn't matter. You know you will think you are stupid if you don't follow your passion because deep down, that's what you want the most. So, when it feels lonely along the way as you are trying your hardest, remember you won't be alone for long.

The people who are ahead of you will never look back and say you are stupid and that you should stop. No, they will be the ones cheering you on! You will be joining them as long as you don't quit!

Meanwhile, the chatter of the people you pass will get louder. Suddenly, everyone has an opinion. Ignoring their feedback is hard, but you need to train yourself to do it. Follow your healthy habits and don't slip.

Remember the story I told you about last Christmas when I gave my mom and brother money and said they needed to grow it so I could match it? Remember I also said if they weren't successful in growing the money, and lost it, I wouldn't match anything, and I wouldn't be back the next year with a money gift?

Before the dinner was even done, my mother was finding ways she was going to fail. My brother was finding ways to succeed and brainstorming. Here is the kicker though, and this goes back to the literal and most important phrase in this book....

"People talk a lot of shit. It's not what they say, it's what they do, how they grow, how they pivot, and the actions they stack that make the difference. PERIOD."

After five months, I called my mom and brother. My brother and his fiancé were behind, hadn't saved, etc., even though he was the one who was so initially excited. My mom, on the other hand, learned acceptance and understanding and got a bonus at work that she put right into her account. She knew deep down that while what I said might have come off as arrogant or me being selfish, the truth in what I wanted her to learn was the nugget. I have zero doubt that my mom will find a way. Also, for all of you out there thinking you live on a budget, she is doing this as a single woman, with a rent payment, a car payment, medical bills, and no help making less than $40,000 a year. So, if she can get resourceful at 60+ years old, imagine what advantages you would have if you just stopped fucking complaining and started getting resourceful.

Here's what I learned at dinner that night: People will be who they are. It's not your job to change them. Your job is to make yourself better. You don't even want the job of changing them or convincing them to see a different aspect of the situation. You have your own shit to get clear on. Other people may get where you are coming from or not. But they can't hold you into paralysis or negativity when you did what you said you were going to do.

The Truth About Toxic People

We've all seen the Facebook posts about how you have to leave toxic people, and that it will be good for you and your life will instantly improve.

Some of that is true.

Your life will look up, and you won't have to deal with all the useless shit people dish out, but there is one thing a lot of people dismiss.

When you distance yourself from toxic people, the sadness doesn't go away and will always be there.

It is not possible to be a human being on earth who doesn't feel pain for a second or a year.

You might feel relief right away from getting your head clear and reclaiming your space, but you will have to live with the pain of sending people away...or people leaving on their own.

Setting boundaries isn't without pain. One of the most painful parts of life is defending boundaries. Yeah, it feels awesome to stand up for yourself, but that doesn't mean it doesn't hurt like a bitch sometimes, too.

The Truth About Social Media

Social media is the trailer park of our country. I hate it. I truly do. It is a completely necessary evil in business today, but I can not tell you how many people are immature, toxic, negative, victimized, scarcity-driven, etc. Especially the bullshit you see people post in memes and quotes and statuses. If Facebook made a rule where you could only post things you have actually done and truly believe in, my feed would have two posts a day, and they would both be making fun of Trump or Kanye.

The fact is social media is the most toxic place on earth. The reason is keyboard courage has turned into keyboard lifestyle, keyboard work ethic, and keyboard ego. I get fucking destroyed by half-truths, untrue statements, personal demons, faults, etc. People try to take what's yours because they simply don't have what it takes to earn what they want themselves or to be true to themselves.

If you truly want to limit toxic exposure, delete social media apps from your phone.

Make it inconvenient to re-download and open and enter your name/password, etc. I promise you; it will truly impact your life positively when you worry less about some internet bridge troll and more about what you actually do in real life that moves you forward.

It is so easy to jump on hate wagons, waste time worrying about other people's problems, and feed into idiots, that you truly make the game easier for people to get ahead of you.

The absolute truth is if you cannot win in this day and age and time in history it is because you never should. It is easier now than ever to win and do what you want and work in the way that you want than it ever has been—due to people's lack of patience and what doing real work entails.

Quit letting toxic people limit your actions.

Social media is NOT work. So fucking cut that dumbshit out. You sitting on your laptop "grinding" and answering comments doesn't do dick. I have built my company faster than anyone before me in my industry because I understand one thing about human beings: they are toxic and lazy. They think "patience" means I should wait for weeks. Those people will get smashed in the long game, and that my friends is the only game that matters.

Getting Through Sadness

Hell, we've all been sad. Even the men who look like zero fucks given, get hit by the shitstorms of life. This is what helps me:

- Ask yourself, why are you sad?
- Is it because you think you're inferior, or that what you have gone through has made you inferior?

It is sad you have lived these circumstances, whatever they are, but they will never go away. You can't remove your history, but you can use your story to give up and tell yourself that you failed somewhere—or you can keep learning and growing from it.

The difference between the people who can keep going and those who can't is that some people will experience sadness and it will ruin them for six months. Others let that sadness ruin them in six minutes.

You will be sad, and it will still hurt, but how long you remain locked in your feelings is up to you.

Why would you choose pain when you can look in the mirror and choose you? When you can leave sadness behind?

And this is the scary AF part I want you to keep in mind:

Even if you go forward, even if you are miles away from where you started in your head...

...You can still go backward if you are not careful to continue to do the work to stay ahead and keep progressing.

You can land right back in that sad slump.

Next year, I will have the validation that I've made the right decision in not letting the client who tried to fuck me over with her tantrum get a reduced rate. She will probably be at another gym having gained all her weight back, and I will be even further down the road in my journey. She will have let her anger and sense of entitlement get in the way, and I will keep pushing the right mindset.

You can't let experiences like these control your day. This is why the fuck-you hour is so important. It allows you to vent and get shit out. You will fully feel the depth of your emotions and then be able to move on. When you are in the middle of the fuck-you hour, a realization hits. You will not change this part of human nature to feel what we have been taught is wrong.

This is part of who you are! This is part of the person in the mirror, and it is more than okay. It is an undeniable truth. There's no reason to be ashamed of it.

It's not a bad thing, to be sad and angry. But what you need to be aware of is the fact that these emotions, when unchecked, are detrimental to happiness.

Every day: own your emotions and own yourself.

Chapter 11: Put Your Darkness to Work

✷✷✷

The best books I read always have a recap section as the last chapter in the back of the book. I consider this to be a cheat sheet so you can quickly reference what you've read as well as know what I want you to walk away with.

I've arranged this book in a particular way, so if you are struggling with a certain part of your darkness; you can jump right into the chapter you need.

Chapter 1 details the fact that we are using pain wrong in our lives. In fact, pain often splits our lives into "before" and "after" moments. But instead of being resentful and angry at the pain, we can use it to push ourselves ahead to become the best versions of ourselves.

This is why I state that "pain can be the defining factor and linchpin in all of us discovering our purpose and the power in that purpose."

Pain can keep you stuck. Pain can push you to punish yourself. Pain can hold you hostage; it can cause you to self-sabotage repeatedly.

Sometimes, we think that we are so special because we have pain. That our pain should give us more pity than other people. Everyone has shit. It's what you do with the shit that matters.

To gain perspective on your pain, make sure that you answer the questions at the end of chapter one. I wrote them for you to help you understand how you are managing your pain...if you have acknowledged it...or are burying it.

Chapter 2 delivers good news for you! If you have an addictive personality, this doesn't have to be a bad realization. You don't have to let your addiction pull you into darkness.

The little-known fact that people don't get is that if you are going to be successful, you have to have a ravenous appetite! You have to be completely self-motivated and accountable. You have to get obsessed and unable to see or want anything else in your life.

When we think of addictions, most of us imagine skid row. A junkie shooting up in an alley somewhere. An alcoholic bellying up to the bar. But we know that we can get addicted to anything that we find irresistible.

Stuff like:

Sugar
Social media
Fast food
Sex

If you have an addictive personality, what got you into trouble can get you out.

Addiction triggers include:

Anger/frustration
Trauma
Diagnosis
Relationships
Conflict
Self-love or lack of self-love

If you are addicted, don't lose hope. I have yet to meet an addict who is satisfied with their lifestyle. They want to get better. And getting better requires a plan you can depend on. Wanting to get better is the secret weapon to reach recovery.

Chapter 3 is a bit proprietary because I gave you exclusive insight into the insane ingredients that are needed for success.

I have a front-row seat as a coach and trainer to watch and help people who are trying to change what they hate about themselves. Without fail, every January, my gyms fill up with people who have the best intentions to lose weight and get fit. I know why people stumble when they get to the finish line.

Most often, they try too hard to disrupt their whole lives. But this is not sustainable. That's why I want you to shoot for small percentage changes. You can make a difference in your life when you switch out your daily candy bar for fruit, for instance. Combine these small shifts with perseverance, and it's not a matter of if, but when you will hit your goals.

This is the shortlist of why we mess ourselves up:

We get tired
We overthink
We are afraid of the unfamiliar
We compare ourselves
We get resentful
We don't realize the power of mental reinforcement

When you are making positive changes in your life, you want to give yourself all the tools necessary to give yourself the best shot at accomplishing your greatness.

Surround yourself with support.

Don't be afraid to interrupt your patterns. This is energizing and creates momentum.

Change your self-talk.
Know you are the problem and the solution.

Finally, the most important lesson to remember is that *you are the only person who can get you to where you want to go.*

Chapter 4 gives you the information you need to customize your path to leave pain behind.

The points to keep handy:

Good information means nothing without action.

You need to move *into* your pain.

Pain is not going to kill you…even if it feels like it will.

You must prioritize yourself. No elite performer has ever hemmed and hawed over what they need to do for themselves. They just do it!

Strive for balance.

We are not here to measure each other's pain.

There are reasons it's so hard to admit our struggles. Revisit this chapter to refamiliarize yourself with them if you need to.

Stop the regret over things that are in the past.

The ingredient in every shit sandwich is pain.
You can stop reliving trauma if you want to.

Moving on and forgiving doesn't mean minimizing pain.

This is the time to decide who and what you will be and do.

You can learn what you really have control over.

Some tools to manage pain:

Meditation
Positive self-talk
Setting boundaries
Writing down what you want

Chapter 5 will put a stop to you comparing yourself to other people once and for all.

1. You don't and never will have enough information about other people to fairly compare yourself.

2. No one else is an expert in you, but you.

3. If you want to play the comparison game, every field must be leveled. Both accomplishments and mistakes must be taken into consideration.

4. Ask yourself, *what am I going to lose by changing what I do?*

5. Allow room for growth.

6. Plan for time to suck.

7. We teach ourselves to hate ourselves.

8. Replace negative self-talk with praise and encouragement.

9. Incorporate the F-U Hour every morning.

10. Refuse immediate gratification.

11. Resist the shame of being human. Too often, we are chastised for having feelings that are very natural and shouldn't be shamed.

Chapter 6 covered the complex ego. You can revisit the table to get the most out of this section.

We are all capable of opening our egos wide to light or darkness.

When you decide your ego direction, reinforce it by positioning your ego in the way you want it to be. I tell people I am the "LeBron James of fat loss."

Egos can protect us, and they can be sick and hurt us. This is why it's critical to be confident as you go after what you want. Or you won't get it.

A person with a healthy ego knows that no one else's opinion matters. Live big, live with no secrets, and you will never have to worry about people getting over on you. When you are on the winning path, there will be pain. Just know that this is normal and you simply need to keep going.

The people in your network need to know it is their job to support you, and you are expected to do the same. If you don't have this kind of network: time to upgrade!

Your job is to be better for you. Like I said, keep your eyes on your bobber. As you are stretching and reaching to be the optimal version of yourself, that's pretty fucking awesome. And as you are changing, you are already perfect. The goal is to improve, even though there is nothing wrong with who you are.

Chapter 7 unveils the secret to abundance that no one talks about.

Unless you let go of scarcity and your self-limiting beliefs, you will stay exactly where you are. Abundance is reciprocal, and the world is made up of givers, takers, and matchers as Adam Dant outlines in his book *Give and Take*.

One of the smartest uses of pain is to give back. When we hurt, nothing feels better than helping someone else.

Chapter 8 gives you the roadmap to getting unstuck. There are very specific things to do when you find yourself in a rut if you want to get out. If you don't want to stay stuck, the only thing that will work is to rip yourself out of this pattern.

Gratitude moves you forward. Even looking for gratitude means you have found it—to your brain anyway.

If you want to move on, ask yourself the questions I listed in this chapter. You will learn why you are stuck, and these reasons are usually deep and buried in our subconscious. Even though you are stuck, you can compartmentalize your emotions through visualization.

Memorize these scarcity patterns and limiting beliefs so you can avoid them:

You are afraid to invest.
Major success is meant for other people.
You don't deserve a better life
You don't have enough willpower to change bad habits
You don't know how to be happy for other people's success.
You compare yourself to everyone else.
You think if other people have a win, it means there is less opportunity for you.
You dig it when other people fail.
When you win, you feel like you have beat everyone.
You give negative reasons when asked why you haven't reached your goals.
It's hard for you to share.

You want to be in charge.
You think of success as a competition.
You don't focus on long-term goals but live in the now.

If you're ready to get unstuck, stop justifying your fears.

Chapter 9 covers what is difficult for a TON of people: asking for and receiving help.

What I want you to remember when you think of this section:

It takes a team of people to accomplish great things.
You make impressions even when you aren't trying to.
Most people don't access this superpower.
What feels good serves us.
Giving is almost selfish, and so is asking for help—this is why it's so damn confusing.
Asking for help requires trust.
Letting someone help you serves them.
You are limited by what you can do yourself.

There are different ways to ask for help. I have given you a number of examples, so if you can't think of how to ask for what you need, flip back through this chapter and reread the list.

We are allowed to ask for help and give ourselves a break.

Regardless of why you are fighting yourself on getting what you need, there is a reason why you are resisting. It's your job to figure out what that is.

Chapter 10 is one of the most valuable chapters in *Darkness Dichotomy* because the conversation comes back to you. To live the life you have dreamed of for years, you have to be true to yourself.

Being true to yourself means you don't give a fuck about what anyone else says or thinks about you.

Your integrity depends on refusing co-dependency and making decisions yourself.

It's hard to let go of the need for approval, but you can do it. And you need to find out why someone else's opinion matters more to you than how you feel about yourself.

Strengthening your mindset is not taking the easy way out.

One of the reasons we can't get over ourselves and bust through to the highest version of ourselves is because we are overcomplicators. We mess everything up with emotions and get in our feels.

If you depend on other people to tell you about yourself, that's toxic! It's intimidating to think of drawing boundaries and kicking those toxic people out, but I want to tell you something that might help you change your mind.

When you leave, when you put distance between yourself and damaging people in your life, you will feel more relief than sadness.

Speaking of sadness, we dive into that, too.

Because we can get stuck in sadness.

But there are ways to get past it. There are ways to live with it without it feeling like it's strangling you alive.

Your life is and should be, all about setting goals for yourself. It should be about pushing yourself and walking through pain. It should be about loving yourself even when it's darker than fuck.

You deserve to have goals.

As you reach for them, you need a guide to kick you in the ass. Consider this book your mindset guide.

Then lay down your foundation.

After you read this book, don't just shove it on a shelf somewhere and let it get dusty. Pull it out again so you can use it the next time life hands you a shit sandwich.

Then use your pain as a catalyst to help you survive.

Use darkness as your motivator to never feel pain as deeply as you have before.

Darkness can push you into the light. You just have to know what to do to get there.

Acknowledgments

My Wife - who sees my struggle, pain, and work ethic and believes in me no matter what life throws in my way. She knows I will win.

My Mom - who did everything she knew how to do to give us a roof and food. She sacrificed years and years of her life to make sure we had the necessities. She is the true definition of love for your kids.

Kyle – who has been my best friend since I was five, who always believed in me and who has supported me in every success and failure. He showed me what a true friend was, even when I didn't deserve it.

Matt - for teaching me everything I knew about my passion and allowing me the opportunity to be 100% me and never giving up on me or what I was capable of. You were the only one who believed in me moving South, and you were the one who pushed me to truly go all-in.

My team- who is incredible and who I work with every single day. Since day one, I have been so blessed to find people who make me better, who care about changing people's lives, and who truly make an impact on thousands of people every single day with their hearts and passion.

My clients – without whom NONE of this would be possible. Our clients support our program, mission, and culture. They allow us the opportunity to live out our dreams every day and support us and our families. The clients who believe in us are truly the secret. I am honored to have you all in my life.

Aaron Nash

About the Author

Aaron Nash is the multi-award-winning gym owner of Platinum Fitness, LLC, one of the fastest-growing 7-figure fitness centers in the United States. He combines the unique experience of group HIIT training workouts, fat loss nutrition programs, and mindset coaching to lead clients to their healthiest results.

Formerly from West Michigan, Aaron now lives in South Florida. He has helped over 150 people lose more than 50 lbs. in five years, equaling a grand total of over 200,000 client lbs. lost. While Aaron and his highly trained staff mentor clients in elevating their mindset, they emphasize implementing the formula to success first in one area of their lives before applying it to other aspects. His method creates consistent, abundant, and balanced lives clients can maintain as they continually challenge themselves.

When Aaron is not running his fitness powerhouses, he enjoys spending time with his wife and kiddo and playing with his bulldogs.

Made in the USA
Monee, IL
01 July 2021